M362 Unit 4

UNDERGRADUATE COMPUTING

Developing concurrent distributed systems

Concurrency in Java: A closer look

Unit 4

This publication forms part of an Open University course M362 *Developing concurrent distributed systems*. Details of this and other Open University courses can be obtained from the Student Registration and Enquiry Service, The Open University, PO Box 197, Milton Keynes MK7 6BJ, United Kingdom: tel. +44 (0)845 300 60 90, email general-enquiries@open.ac.uk

Alternatively, you may visit the Open University website at http://www.open.ac.uk where you can learn more about the wide range of courses and packs offered at all levels by The Open University.

To purchase a selection of Open University course materials visit http://www.ouw.co.uk, or contact Open University Worldwide, Michael Young Building, Walton Hall, Milton Keynes MK7 6AA, United Kingdom for a brochure. tel. +44 (0)1908 858793; fax +44 (0)1908 858787; email ouw-customer-services@open.ac.uk

The Open University
Walton Hall
Milton Keynes
MK7 6AA

First published 2008.

Edited and designed by The Open University.

Typeset by The Open University.

Printed and bound in the United Kingdom by Hobbs the Printers, Totton, Hampshire.

ISBN 978 0 7492 1592 7

1.1

The paper used in this publication contains pulp sourced from forests independently certified to the Forest Stewardship Council® (FSC®) principles criteria. Chain of custody certification allows the pulp from these forests to be tracked to the end use (see www.fsc-uk.org).

CONTENTS

1 Introduction   5

   1.1   The aims of this unit   5

2 The Java Virtual Machine   6

   2.1   Virtual machines   6

   2.2   JVM specifications and implementations   9

   2.3   The Java memory model   13

   2.4   Threading models   22

3 Concurrency utilities   25

   3.1   Java's limitations   25

   3.2   Concurrent collections   26

   3.3   Atomic variables   31

   3.4   Locks   33

   3.5   Synchronisers   37

   3.6   Task scheduling   40

4 Thread safety   43

   4.1   Synchronise access to shared mutable data   43

   4.2   Avoid unnecessary synchronisation   45

   4.3   Always call wait inside a loop   46

   4.4   Do not depend on the thread scheduler   47

   4.5   Document thread safety   47

   4.6   Summary of advice on code writing   50

5 Summary   52

Glossary   54

References   57

Index   58

M362 COURSE TEAM

Affiliated to The Open University unless otherwise stated.

Chair, author and academic editor
Janet van der Linden

Authors
Anton Dil

Brendan Quinn

Michel Wermelinger

Critical readers and testers
Henryk Krajinski

Barbara Segal

Mark Thomas

Richard Walker

Yijun Yu

External assessor
Aad van Moorsel, Newcastle University

Software development
Ivan Dunn, Consultant

Course management
Linda Landsberg

Carrie Lewis

Barbara Poniatowska

Julia White

Media development staff
Ian Blackham, Editor

Sarah Gamman, Contracts Executive

Jennifer Harding, Editor

Phillip Howe, Media Assistant

Martin Keeling, Media Assistant

Callum Lester, Software Developer

Andy Seddon, Media Project Manager

Sue Stavert, Technical Testing Team

Andrew Whitehead, Designer and Graphic Artist

Thanks are due to the Desktop Publishing Unit of the Faculty of Mathematics, Computing and Technology.

1 Introduction

In the previous two units we saw how threads can be created in Java, the states a thread can be in, and the general problems that concurrent applications may have, such as deadlock and starvation. In this unit we go into more detail about the support that Java provides for building multithreaded applications.

We will start with a closer look at the Java Virtual Machine (JVM), the infrastructure that allows a Java program to be compiled on one platform and then be executed on a different one. This is very convenient for developing and distributing applications across multiple platforms in a networked world. To achieve such platform independence, the JVM designers had to specify an abstract model for the handling of data and threads, but left the details to each platform-specific JVM implementation. We will see in Section 2 the implications of this for the behaviour of multithreaded programs and their portability across platforms.

Section 3 looks at the limitations of Java's original support for concurrency and how Java 1.5 has addressed them. (Note, the reason Java 1.5 remains important to us, is that this was the version in which a number of concurrency issues were addressed.) In particular, we will see how the package `java.util.concurrent` has introduced more flexible monitors, higher-level utilities to coordinate threads, and collection classes that behave better under concurrent access. All this allows developers to use code developed by concurrency experts, instead of spending time reinventing the wheel.

In the previous unit we discussed generic concurrency mechanisms and how they seek to guarantee a program's safety property. Section 4 continues this discussion with a closer look at concurrency issues, in particular at thread safety. A class is said to be thread-safe if it behaves as intended even when multiple concurrent threads access it in an uncoordinated way. We will see that there are various levels of thread safety, possibly requiring some 'cooperation' between the thread-safe class and its callers, and we provide some generic advice on how to write thread-safe classes.

1.1 The aims of this unit

This unit will discuss:

▶ what the JVM is (Section 2);

▶ the impact of platform and the JVM on the behaviour of concurrent programs (Section 2);

▶ how to make use of some of the more sophisticated concurrency utilities introduced by Java 1.5 (Section 3);

▶ the levels of thread safety (Section 4);

▶ common pitfalls to avoid when writing thread-safe classes (Section 4).

This unit involves reading together with exercises. There are also a number of practical activities which require you to do some programming.

2 The Java Virtual Machine

In this section we look at the 'heart' of any Java system: its virtual machine. We start with a brief introduction to what virtual machines are and why they are useful. We then look at the Java Virtual Machine (JVM) in particular, including its memory model and the interplay between Java's and the platform's threading models. Although the exact details of the JVM are beyond the scope of this course, a basic knowledge of Java's 'inner workings' is useful in order to understand why programs may not behave the way we might expect them to.

2.1 Virtual machines

As we have seen in *Unit 2*, Section 2, a frequent approach to developing a program is to write it in some high-level programming language and then compile it into the low-level machine code that is directly executable by the hardware's CPU. As we have also seen in that section, the execution of a program usually requires calls to be made to the operating system (OS) to access devices. Therefore, a compiled program can run only on the hardware and operating system for which it was compiled. As stated in *Unit 2*, Section 2, the combination of a particular hardware architecture with a particular operating system is called a platform. For example, a program compiled for the Windows/Intel platform will not run on a Linux/Intel or a Windows/Motorola platform. In fact, a program compiled for a particular version of Windows with a particular Motorola chip may not run on some other Windows/Motorola combination, though we will usually omit specific CPU and OS details for simplicity.

Compiling a program on a specific platform has the advantage of making its execution very fast but has the disadvantage of requiring the user to have exactly the same platform as the developer. If we wish the same program to run on different platforms, we have to make different versions of the program (e.g. because the graphical interfaces are different for different operating systems), compile them with different platform-specific compilers, and keep track of all changes to keep the various versions consistent. This is not a simple endeavour.

You may come across other meanings of 'virtual machine', but this is the one relevant for this course.

One solution to this problem is to use a **virtual machine** (**VM**). A virtual machine is an abstract computing device that implements in software a hypothetical (hence the adjective *virtual*) platform. The crux of the idea is to compile programs for the virtual platform, and implement the virtual machine on top of various concrete platforms. In that way, there is only one version of the source program, which is compiled only once (into the virtual machine's machine code), and then executed on any platform for which the virtual machine has been implemented.

To specify a virtual machine, you need to state which instructions it accepts, what the result of executing them will be, and how code and data are organised in memory. Specifying a virtual machine is a very hard task. On the one hand, the specification has to be 'open' enough that it can be implemented on different platforms; on the other hand, it has to be sufficiently detailed to ensure that any program behaves in the same way, regardless of the platform on which it runs.

The implementation of a virtual machine consists of an **interpreter**, i.e. a program that executes another program. The virtual machine interpreter takes a program written in the virtual machine's code, which is the outcome of the compilation process, and exccutes the instructions according to the definition prescribed by the virtual machine specification. The advantage of the virtual machine concept is that the compiler and interpreter may run on different platforms. Figure 1 shows this for the case of Java.

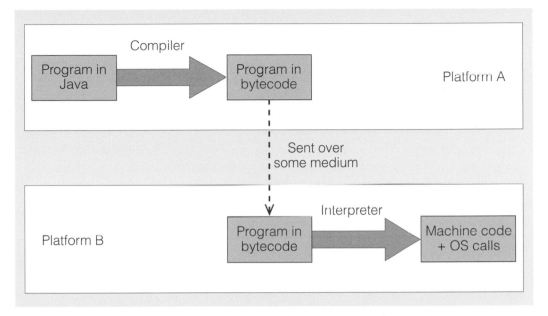

Figurc 1   A Java program is compiled on one platform and executed on another one

To sum up, a virtual machine and a computer architecture both define operations and memory, and the way in which execution of the former affects the latter. The difference is that a virtual machine is implemented in software, using an interpreter, whereas a computer architecture is implemented in hardwarc, using a CPU. In fact, a CPU can be regarded as an interpreter implemented on a chip.

It is important to note that in many texts, including this unit, the term 'virtual machine' refers sometimes to the abstract platform-independent specification and sometimes to a concrete platform-specific implementation. This should be clear from the context; e.g. in the phrase 'the virtual machine executes the instructions' we are referring to some implementation of the virtual machine specification.

Other interpreters

Interpreters are not used just in the context of virtual machines. Several simple languages, especially for interactive 'one-off' use, are directly interpreted, instead of being compiled into virtual machine code or machine code. For example, before the widespread use of graphical user interfaces, users interacted with the operating system through textual command languages to move from one directory to another, list files within a directory, copy and delete files, etc. The Microsoft DOS and Unix shell commands are such an example: they are directly interpreted, i.e. executed, instead of being compiled into some intermediate form. Database query languages, like SQL, and simple programming languages, like old versions of BASIC, may also be interpreted. Scripting languages like JavaScript (used in M150) are usually interpreted. As a final example, the OUWorkspace tool used in M255 is built on top of BeanShell, which interprets Java source code directly.

BeanShell.

The Java designers decided to adopt the virtual machine concept for their language. A Java compiler translates a Java program into **bytecode**, which is the machine code of the **Java Virtual Machine** (**JVM**). A Java interpreter (i.e. an implementation of the JVM) then cxccutes the bytecode on a particular platform, possibly different from the platform on which the program was compiled. One of the reasons why Java is so popular is the availability of interpreters for many platforms, enabling Java programs to run on PDAs, mobile phones and desktop machines of various manufacturers and using various operating systems. This has been succinctly put as 'write once, run anywhere'.

Figure 1 shows that process, emphasising that compilers as well as interpreters can be seen as translators: a compiler translates a high-level textual language (Java in this case) into a low-level binary format (bytecode), and an interpreter translates platform-independent code (bytecode) into platform-dependent machine code and operating system calls.

The Z-machine.

Famous virtual machines

The virtual machine concept was invented long before Java. Two of the best known examples are the pseudomachine of the Pascal system developed at the University of California, San Diego, in the late 1970s, and the Warren Abstract Machine developed by David H. Warren in the early 1980s to efficiently execute Prolog programs. As is the case for Java, those virtual machines helped make Pascal (a procedural language) and Prolog (a logic-based language used in artificial intelligence) very popular.

But according to Nick Montfort (2005, pp. 126–7), the first commercial implementation of the virtual machine concept was the Z-machine developed in 1979 by Infocom, a US company that sold text-based adventure games. Using a virtual machine allowed Infocom to sell each game for several of the distinct hardware architectures existing in the 1980s (Atari, Apple, Commodore, etc.). The Z-machine is still in use today and may well be the virtual machine that has been implemented for the widest range of platforms.

Advantages and disadvantages

There are several advantages in using virtual machines. The foremost has already been given: if an organisation wants to develop and market n different applications for p different platforms, instead of developing and compiling $n \times p$ slightly different programs, the organisation distributes only n applications, assuming there is a virtual machine implementation for each platform. Overall, only $n + p$ programs are needed instead of $n \times p$.

A further advantage is that a program compiled to virtual machine code is usually smaller than if it were compiled to machine code. This is useful for running programs on small devices and for distributing programs across networks. The reason for this is that the instruction set of a virtual machine is usually at a higher level of abstraction than machine code. For example, the JVM accepts an instruction to invoke a method on an object. By contrast, the execution of this single instruction on a particular platform will typically require many machine code instructions: the polymorphic nature of Java methods makes it necessary to find out at runtime what the class of the object is so that the correct method is invoked, and, if the method is synchronised, the lock has to be acquired. This additional work will need to be done automatically by any JVM implementation, using the instruction set of the platform it is running on.

A further advantage is that multiple languages can be compiled to the same virtual machine. This facilitates the development of heterogeneous systems in which components are written in different languages, making the best usage of each language's features. It also promotes the creation of new languages with novel programming features, as language designers only have to develop a compiler which translates from the new language into code for some existing virtual machine. Programs

Programming languages for the JVM.

developed with the new language can automatically be run on all platforms for which the virtual machine has been implemented.

The main disadvantage of virtual machines is that virtual machine code is executed by software (i.e. the application's code is interpreted by a virtual machine implementation for a particular platform). If a program is compiled into virtual machine code and executed on top of a virtual machine, it will run much more slowly than if it had been compiled into machine code and executed directly. However, improvements in language-processing technology have led to better performance of virtual machine implementations. One of those technologies is **just-in-time** (**JIT**) **compilation**: a program's virtual machine code, instead of being interpreted, is translated into machine code the first time the program is executed. Usually, the overhead imposed by runtime compilation only pays off if the code being compiled is executed multiple times, e.g. if it is the code of a frequently called method. Otherwise, the time to compile the virtual machine code and execute the generated machine code might be larger than the time to interpret the virtual machine code.

A further problem, that is not unique to virtual machines, is the general issue of backwards compatibility. In the same way that a file written with a certain version of a word processor might not be readable with a previous version, or that programs compiled for a certain operating system or CPU cannot be run on a previous version (e.g. the Pentium versus the x486 processors, all from Intel), a program compiled for a certain virtual machine version might not run on a platform for which only a different virtual machine version is implemented.

Finally, you should be aware that the existence of a virtual machine for a given platform does not hide the limitations of the platform. For example, even if two virtual machine implementations, one for a desktop machine and another for a PDA, are compatible, an application written with the memory and graphical interface of a desktop machine in mind might not work properly when run on a PDA. We will return to this point at the end of the next section.

SAQ 1

Summarise the advantages and disadvantages of using virtual machines.

ANSWER...

The main disadvantage of using virtual machines is the slower execution speed of the program, compared with compiling it directly to machine code that is interpreted by the CPU. Moreover, virtual machines are also subject to backward compatibility problems and to the limitations of the various platforms.

The advantages are that the generated virtual machine code is smaller than the corresponding machine code and can be executed on various platforms without requiring any changes, making it easier for organisations to develop applications for a wide user base. Moreover, virtual machines facilitate the development of applications written in multiple languages and promote the creation of new languages.

2.2 JVM specifications and implementations

The JVM specification defines a platform-independent binary format, called the `class` file format. Such a format defines the representation of a class or interface, including the method code (a sequence of JVM instructions operating on typed values). The JVM instruction set includes not only the usual low-level arithmetic, logical and control instructions, such as 'add two integers' and 'jump to address X', but also high-level instructions that mirror Java features, such as invoking methods, raising exceptions, creating new objects and entering and exiting monitors (i.e. synchronised methods).

Besides the instruction set, the JVM specification also defines the memory areas that have to be managed during runtime. Some areas are allocated to the whole JVM, others are allocated to each thread. Those areas allocated to the JVM are created when the JVM starts up, and removed when it exits; those areas allocated to a thread are created and deleted when the thread is created and terminated (see *Unit 2*, Figure 12). The principal memory areas are as follows (see also *Unit 2*, Section 6):

▶ a program counter register to hold the address of the instruction being executed;

▶ a stack of activation frames;

▶ a heap to hold the objects;

▶ a method area to hold the code of the methods.

However, the JVM specification does not prescribe how those areas are actually mapped to the hardware's memory (cache, RAM, disk, etc.). For example, the heap does not have to be a contiguous area and the stack of activation frames may be just a stack of pointers to records dynamically allocated and deallocated on the heap. This freedom makes it possible to implement a JVM as efficiently as possible for a given platform, be it a mobile phone with limited memory and slower CPU speed, or a powerful workstation.

Exercise 1

Which of the above memory areas are allocated to each thread, and which are allocated to the whole JVM?

Discussion...

Since each thread executes independently, each one needs a program counter and a stack of activation frames, in order to keep track of which methods have been called and which instruction of the current method is being executed. However, the objects and their code are shared by all threads, and therefore the heap and method area are created on JVM start-up and allocated to the whole JVM.

One of the goals of Sun Microsystems, when creating Java, was to facilitate the development of software for networked consumer devices such as mobile phones and TV set-top boxes. The virtual machine concept was adopted because it allowed for compact and platform-independent code to be sent across networks. For this to be possible, the JVM includes a **class loader** that is able to load a `class` file into the method area of an already running program. Classes are loaded into the JVM only when they are needed (e.g. to instantiate an object), which helps to keep memory usage to the strictly necessary because classes that are not used in a particular execution of the program are not loaded – the activity shows this.

Activity 4.1

Class loader example.

To the class loader, it is irrelevant whether the required class is stored locally or whether it has to be fetched across a network from some remote server. All the class loader needs to know is the name of the class and a set of possible locations where it can search for the class. When the Java interpreter starts up, there is an initial set of locations where it looks for classes – usually the current directory and the directory where Java's standard libraries are stored. But this initial set of locations can be extended at runtime so that a Java program can load new classes from locations it never 'knew' before. How this is done and what it can be used for will be shown in *Unit 7*.

An additional requirement for the JVM was that devices receiving code should have some guarantee that it is safe to run that code. This led to the inclusion of a **bytecode verifier** in the virtual machine. The verifier scans the bytecode before it is executed, checking for certain kinds of error, such as using addresses outside the allocated memory areas, jumping out of the current method (i.e. without using a 'return' instruction), or breaking the type system. A correct Java compiler will not generate bytecode with such errors, but a malicious developer might have tampered with a compiler or the generated code. Unsuspecting users running such code could face disastrous consequences if it were not for the bytecode verifier. However, keep in mind that the verifier does not check for all kinds of error. *Units 7* and *10* will return to this issue of 'trusting' the integrity of the code about to be executed.

In Java, there are constructors to create new objects but there are no destructors to delete objects. Instead, developers rely on the JVM implementing an automatic **garbage collection** mechanism that reclaims the memory occupied by unused objects from the heap, to keep memory usage as low as possible. The JVM specification does not prescribe any particular garbage collection algorithm.

Object-oriented garbage collection

In employing automatic garbage collection, Java follows the same approach as Smalltalk, one of the early object-oriented languages and still one of the most elegant languages ever invented. On the other hand, C++, an object-oriented extension of C, has no automatic garbage collection: developers have to explicitly call `delete anObject` when object `anObject` is no longer needed.

JVM implementations may allow the user to pass parameters to the Java interpreter in order to set some execution options, e.g. the garbage collection policy to use, the size of the stack area for each thread, or whether JIT compilation is turned on. This can have a dramatic impact on the performance of the application, especially if it has to deal with hundreds or thousands of threads. Such fine-tuning of performance is, of course, platform- and JVM-specific.

JVM implementations and editions

In addition to providing a specification of the JVM, Sun Microsystems also provides concrete implementations for several platforms, including Solaris and Windows, for desktop systems. As said before, the specification must be sufficiently precise to provide an unambiguous meaning for the instruction set (i.e. what the instructions exactly do when executed), and yet be sufficiently 'open' to achieve independence from platform-specific technologies and to let implementers use the current state-of-the-art technology when targeting a specific platform or usage pattern.

As an example, the JVM specification does not prescribe how the bytecode is to be executed, in particular whether it is to be interpreted, or compiled to machine code. Sun Microsystems' own virtual machine implementations show how this freedom can be put to use, through a mixture of interpretation and compilation: the virtual machine analyses the code as it runs, to detect any so-called 'hot spots', i.e. regions of code that have performance bottlenecks. It can then apply different kinds of optimisation, such as JIT compilation, to those hot spots.

As a further example of this flexible approach, Sun Microsystems provides the Java HotSpot Client VM, designed to start up quickly and to use as little memory as possible, and the Java HotSpot Server VM that executes code as quickly as possible, possibly at the expense of consuming more memory.

JVM implementations.

Exercise 2

Based on your knowledge of client–server systems, can you give some reasons for having two different virtual machines for clients and servers?

Discussion..

Servers usually have large amounts of memory and should only be rebooted occasionally; a small memory footprint and quick start-up time is therefore not essential, but execution speed is, in order to deal with a large load of client requests.

Sun Microsystems aims for Java to run on all kinds of different machines, from powerful web servers to small devices like PDAs and mobile phones. To address the wide range of hardware architectures and application needs, the Java Platform is issued in three editions:

▶   Java Platform, Enterprise Edition (Java EE),

▶   Java Platform, Standard Edition (Java SE),

▶   Java Platform, Micro Edition (Java ME).

Block 2 of this course deals with the Java EE.

Each edition is basically a set of tools, libraries, API specifications, etc. that are considered relevant for a certain kind of system: enterprise applications with web front-ends and database back-ends (Java EE); simple desktop applications (Java SE); and applications for small devices (Java ME). The Java EE and Java SE both use the same JVM specification, but the Java ME requires the virtual machine to be adapted to fit the reduced processing capabilities and memory of small devices.

Due to the wide range of capabilities of the various devices for which the Java ME was designed, Sun Microsystems decided to specify only a core set of features that all implementations must exhibit, leaving other features – such as supporting threads (and hence the `Object` methods `wait` and `notify`) – as optional.

Each vendor providing a Java ME implementation has to define a *configuration*, the set of language features and libraries that the implementation supports, together with any consequent changes to the JVM specification. The configuration has, of course, to cover at least the core Java ME features.

Java Platform, Micro Edition

As a further example of optional features in the Java ME, some small hardware architectures may only support up to 16-bit integers, and Java programs for such devices therefore cannot use the `float`, `long` or `double` data types. Moreover, several less used or redundant methods were removed from library classes and some of the Java SE libraries were eliminated entirely, including, for example, the Abstract Windows Toolkit, a full-fledged platform-independent graphical user API.

Sun Microsystems provides two Java ME configurations, the Connected Device Configuration (CDC) and the Connected Limited Device Configuration (CLDC). The latter targets devices with 16-bit processors, limited battery power and network bandwidth, and 160 KB to 512 KB of available memory for Java; while the CDC targets devices with higher specification CPUs and more memory. Sun Microsystems also provides a reference virtual machine implementation for CLDC, the Kilobyte VM (KVM), with 'Kilobyte' referring to the small memory requirements of the virtual machine. A higher-performance implementation, the CLDC Hotspot VM, is also available: it is specifically developed for ARM (Advanced RISC Machine) processors with at least 512 KB of memory.

Exercise 3

It is often said that Java applications can be described as 'write once, run anywhere'. Comment on the validity of this statement in the context of the various Java editions and implementations discussed above.

Discussion...

Although the usage of a single language, a good set of predefined libraries and a virtual machine greatly facilitates the development of applications that can be executed on a wide range of platforms, the quote should not be read as if *every* Java application can run on *any* platform. In fact, only applications that restrict themselves to the language features and libraries that are common to the three Java Platform editions can be expected to run everywhere. However, such applications are probably of small interest, because applications usually have a certain kind of device (server, mobile phone, etc.) in mind. The quote should thus be understood only within the context of a given edition (or configuration of the Java ME).

2.3   The Java memory model

Although the JVM specification allows considerable freedom in how actual implementations execute instructions and store data, some constraints must be imposed in order to guarantee that multithreaded programs will work correctly. Without such constraints, JVM implementations might, in the interests of performance, optimise code execution and data storage in such a way that values updated by a thread are not properly propagated to other threads. We will first see an example of the problem and then look at the restrictions Java imposes to avoid it.

Code reordering

For maximum execution speed, variables and constants being operated on are held in registers, which are the fastest type of memory but have limited storage capacity (*Unit 2*, Section 2). Transfer of data between registers and main memory should be done only when absolutely needed and, in order to achieve this, the sequence of instructions may be reordered so as to reuse values that are already in registers. Consider the following pseudocode, where E is some complex expression not depending on y:

> $x = 2 + 3;$ $f = E;$ $y = x + 2;$

Executing the code in the given order could result in the registers containing the values x and 2 being overwritten while computing f, so the values would need to be reloaded in order to execute the final statement. It may be more efficient to compute y before f:

> $x = 2 + 3;$ $y = x + 2;$ $f = E;$

Such code reordering is done routinely by compilers and microprocessors to improve performance. Any reordering done will, of course, not change the semantics of sequential programs. In the second pseudocode listing, the first two statements will not be reordered: assigning to y before the computation of the value of x would change the result of the sequential program. However, for concurrent programs the compiler has, in general, no way to know beforehand how many threads will exist and which parts of the code they will execute concurrently. Reordering is therefore generally performed as if the program were sequential, which may lead to unexpected results during concurrent execution.

The JSR 133 (Java Memory Model) FAQ.

Consider the following code adapted from Manson and Goetz's *JSR 133 (Java Memory Model) FAQ* (2004):

```java
public class Reordering
{
  int x, y;
  public void writer()
  {
    x = 1;
    y = 2;
  }

  public void reader()
  {
    int ry = y;
    int rx = x;
    System.out.println("ry is " + ry);
    System.out.println("rx is " + rx);
  }
}
```

Within each method, the assignments can be reordered without affecting the values of the variables at the start and end of the method.

Exercise 4

Consider a sequential execution of the above code, in which the `writer` method is executed before the `reader` method, but in which the statements within the body of each method may be reordered. List all the possible orderings of the assignment statements and write down the output that results from the execution. Then do the same for the case where `reader` is executed before `writer`.

Discussion...

If `writer` is executed before `reader`, then any of the following assignment orderings results in `ry is 2` and `rx is 1` being printed.

▶   x = 1;   y = 2;   ry = y;   rx = x;

▶   y = 2;   x = 1;   ry = y;   rx = x;

▶   x = 1;   y = 2;   rx = x;   ry = y;

▶   y = 2;   x = 1;   rx = x;   ry = y;

If `reader` is executed before `writer`, then any of the following orderings results in `ry is 0` and `rx is 0` being printed, i.e. the default values for `int`.

▶   ry = y;   rx = x;   x = 1;   y = 2;

▶   ry = y;   rx = x;   y = 2;   x = 1;

▶   rx = x;   ry = y;   x = 1;   y = 2;

▶   rx = x;   ry = y;   y = 2;   x = 1;

Exercise 4 shows that, for the `Reordering` example, the result of each method is independent of the order of the assignments within that method.

The next two exercises explore the situation where each method is executed by a different thread. We will consider only interleaved executions and see that results different from the sequential execution can occur. The case where one thread completely executes one method before the other thread executes the other method is the same as the sequential execution (by a single thread) in the previous exercise.

Exercise 5

Suppose that the `reader` and `writer` methods are executed by different threads, leading to possible interleaving. Assuming that there is no reordering of the statements within the methods, list all the possible interleaved execution sequences and write down the output which results.

Discussion...

Without code reordering, there are only four possible interleaved sequences, all of them resulting in `ry` is 0 and `rx` is 1.

▶   x = 1;   ry = y;   rx = x;   y = 2;

▶   x = 1;   ry = y;   y = 2;   rx = x;

▶   ry = y;   x = 1;   rx = x;   y = 2;

▶   ry = y;   x = 1;   y = 2;   rx = x;

Note that in the four interleaved sequences, one thread is carrying out the assignments to x and y, while the other is carrying out the assignments to `ry` and `rx`. The result is always the same because, whatever the interleaving of the two threads, y is always read before being written, and x is always written before being read.

Exercise 6

Now consider an interleaved execution where code reordering can also occur. List all the possible execution sequences in addition to those already given in Exercise 5, and write down the resulting output.

Discussion...

With interleaved execution *and* reordering of the assignments, the following sequences are also possible.

```
1   x = 1;   rx = x;   y = 2;   ry = y;
2   x = 1;   rx = x;   ry = y;   y = 2;
3   y = 2;   ry = y;   x = 1;   rx = x;
4   y = 2;   ry = y;   rx = x;   x = 1;
5   y = 2;   rx = x;   x = 1;   ry = y;
6   y = 2;   rx = x;   ry = y;   x = 1;
7   ry = y;   y = 2;   rx = x;   x = 1;
8   ry = y;   y = 2;   x = 1;   rx = x;
9   rx = x;   x = 1;   ry = y;   y = 2;
10  rx = x;   x = 1;   y = 2;   ry = y;
11  rx = x;   y = 2;   x = 1;   ry = y;
12  rx = x;   y = 2;   ry = y;   x = 1;
```

The following table gives the possible results.

Table 1   Results arising from interleaved execution

Sequence	Value of ry	Value of rx
1, 3	2	1
2, 8	0	1
4, 5, 6, 10, 11, 12	2	0
7, 9	0	0

As the table shows, each variable can have two final values, depending on whether it is written before it is read, or not. With code reordering and interleaved execution, all value combinations are possible. Three of the combinations were already possible just with code reordering (Exercise 4) or just with interleaving (Exercise 5), but the two things together generate a new output: `ry is 2` and `rx is 0`.

This result is quite counter-intuitive because it could be assumed from looking at the method bodies that if the value 2 is observed for `ry`, then x must have been assigned 1, but that assumption does not take instruction reordering into account. However, it is worth noting that it is unlikely that assignments are reordered in simple examples like this one, because there is no performance gain to be obtained from such reordering.

To sum up, the problem is that, due to code reordering, the order in which values are written by one thread may be 'incompatible' with the order in which they are read by the other thread.

Mutual exclusion

The main problem with the previous example is that it exhibits race conditions (*Unit 3*, Section 2): the two threads are racing for access to x and y, and the output depends on the exact sequential or interleaved order of statements. Code reordering just compounds this problem as there may be more possible execution sequences than are apparent from the source code. We have seen in *Unit 3*, Section 3, that imposing mutually excluded access to shared data avoids some race conditions.

In our example, if the `writer` and `reader` methods are `synchronized`, the traces shown in Exercises 5 and 6 cannot occur because the synchronisation imposes an ordering between the writes and the reads: either the data is written before being read, or vice versa. But there would remain a race condition: the threads are racing to obtain the lock on the `Reordering` object. The order in which they obtain it will dictate the output (see the discussion of Exercise 4). Mutual exclusion can address the interleaved access to shared data but not which thread should get access first.

Exercise 7

How would you change the `Reordering` class so that the values are output only after `writer` has initialised them?

Discussion..

A solution is to add a variable that signals whether the initialisation has been done. The code becomes:

```
public class Reordering
{
  int x, y;
  boolean initialised = false;

  public synchronized void writer()
  {
    x = 1;
    y = 2;
    initialised = true;
    notifyAll();
  }
```

```
public synchronized void reader()
{
  while (! initialised)
  {
    wait();
  }
  int ry = y;
  int rx = x;
  System.out.println("ry is " + ry);
  System.out.println("rx is " + rx);
  }
}
```

Although it may not be a solution for all race conditions, mutual exclusion is a solution to the subtle problems that code reordering may introduce. It effectively imposes a sequential execution of the accesses, and, as we have seen, code reordering is applied in such a way that it does not have any side effects in a sequential context.

Volatile variables

There is another problem, besides code reordering, which can lead to incorrect behaviour of concurrent programs. Unfortunately, it is a problem that cannot be solved by mutual exclusion and therefore another mechanism is needed. Here we look into that problem and see a Java language construct – the `volatile` keyword – that addresses it.

As we have seen in *Unit 2*, Section 2, there is a hierarchy of memory used during the execution of a program, with values being copied from the slow persistent memory (disk storage) at the bottom of the hierarchy to the fast transient memory (registers) at the top of the hierarchy, where values can be updated by the CPU, and then copied back to persistent storage. Moreover, some of the memory may be shared across processes. For example, in shared-memory multiprocessor architectures, each processor has its own cache, but main memory is shared. It is important to maintain caches and main memory to be always consistent with each other so that the various processors work with the same values for the same variables.

A multithreaded program running on a single processor may give rise to similar problems of consistency. Although there is only one cache and one set of CPU registers, each thread makes a copy of the register values when it is pre-empted or has to wait on some event, and copies them back into the registers when it is rescheduled, thus enabling it to resume computation at the point where it left off. So, in a multithreaded program the consistency of shared variables must be maintained across the various 'thread-local' registers and the main memory in the same way that a shared-memory multiprocessor architecture must maintain consistency between multiple caches and the main memory.

The following example (in which one thread sets a flag to terminate another thread) demonstrates incorrect runtime behaviour resulting from the inconsistency of shared variable values across different forms of memory.

```
class MyThread extends Thread
{
  private boolean done = false;

  public void run()
  {
    while (! done)
    {
      // do something
      try
      {
        Thread.sleep(100);
      }
      catch (InterruptedException e)
      {
        // do something
      }
    }
  }

  public void finish()
  {
    done = true;
  }
}
```

Imagine the following code executed by a thread T.

```
// do something             // thread T executes
MyThread my = new MyThread();   // thread T creates thread my
my.start();                 // thread my starts running
// do something             // thread T allows new thread to progress
my.finish();                // thread T tells thread my to finish
```

The `MyThread` methods are called by two threads, T and my. Typically, thread my reads the value of done from main memory into a register and then uses a kind of 'jump on non-zero' machine code instruction to skip the loop if the register has the value true. When thread T calls finish, it sets the value of a register to true and then copies the register to the memory location of done. It is easy to see that thread my will never terminate if it does not reread the value of done from main memory into its register whenever the loop condition has to be evaluated. We have therefore obtained incorrect behaviour if the copies of the shared variable done held by my and T are not consistent.

Note that there is no mutual exclusion problem in this case because reading and setting boolean variables are atomic operations in Java.

Exercise 8

Even if the problem in the above example did involve mutual exclusion, why cannot both methods be synchronised?

Discussion...

If run and finish are synchronized methods, the lock on my would only be released when run terminates. Method run can only terminate if finish is called, but T cannot obtain the lock on my. Hence my.run() gets into an infinite loop and T is blocked forever.

To handle cases such as this, Java introduced **volatile variables**. By definition, they are always written and read from *shared* memory to guarantee that any change made by a thread is visible to other threads. In the above example, simply including the `volatile` keyword before `boolean` will ensure that `my` always reads the most up-to-date value of `done` from memory.

Knowing that shared non-volatile variables may have multiple inconsistent copies across threads leads us to reconsider the example used in Exercises 4, 5 and 6. We implicitly assumed that just by serialising the method calls, the changes made to `x` and `y` by the thread running `writer` are necessarily visible to the thread running the method `reader`. From what we know so far, the `synchronized` keyword serves to impose mutual exclusion and the `volatile` keyword serves to impose value consistency across threads. Hence, it seems that we would always need to have synchronised code *and* volatile data to guarantee the correct behaviour of multithreaded programs. So why are volatile variables only occasionally necessary? For the answer, we must step back again to shared memory hardware.

Memory barriers

We have seen that multiple processors with local caches and a global shared memory give rise to the problem of guaranteeing consistency of values. This led to the introduction of defined **memory models** for those architectures, specifying when **memory barriers** should be set up. A memory barrier restores consistency in one of two ways – flushing the cache or invalidating the cache – depending on the circumstances. A cache flush copies updated values from the cache to the shared memory in order for them to become visible to other processors. A cache invalidation forces values in main memory updated by other processors to be reloaded into the local cache.

The safest solution might appear to be to have a memory barrier for each access to a variable, in particular to flush the cached value whenever it is written, and to invalidate the cached value whenever it is read. The problem with this 'solution' is that it defeats the whole purpose of caches, namely to reduce the number of accesses to the slower main memory. The difficulty in defining a memory model is to come up with the conditions for imposing memory barriers which are both necessary and sufficient: necessary to guarantee the correct behaviour of the multiprocessor applications, and sufficient in the sense that any further conditions are redundant and could reduce the performance of the applications.

In the case of Java, a memory model is a set of conditions that have to be obeyed by JVM implementers in order to guarantee that a value written by the currently running thread will be visible to other threads, and, vice versa, that values previously written by other threads are visible to the running one. Java was the first language to incorporate a memory model for consistent concurrency semantics across multiple platforms. This was an ambitious undertaking that proved to be quite difficult, with various subtle flaws being discovered over time, like the possibility of a thread observing two different values for a `final` field. The memory model was much improved in Java 1.5; developers should therefore be aware that using versions prior to Java 1.5 might lead to subtle occasional bugs in some JVMs. The details of Java's memory model are mostly of concern for JVM implementers, but the main points which developers should be aware of are:

1   synchronisation imposes not only mutual exclusion but also memory barriers;

2   code is not reordered across memory barriers;

3   accesses to volatile variables also impose memory barriers.

Regarding the first point, the basic idea is that on acquisition of a lock the values in a process's registers will be updated with those in memory (cache invalidation), and on release of the lock any values stored in registers will be written to memory (cache flush).

However, this will guarantee correct behaviour only if the threads acquire or release the *same* lock. If threads execute code that is synchronised on different objects, then no ordering of the corresponding memory barriers can be assumed, and hence there is no guarantee that any updates by one thread are propagated to the other ones. To put it more concretely, if thread *A* releases the lock on object *O*, and thread *B* acquires the lock on object *P*, the JVM provides no guarantee whatsoever that the values updated by *A* will be visible to *B*. The imposition of memory barriers as part of synchronisation explains why if threads *A* and *B* are executing synchronised code on the same object, the values updated by one of them will be visible to the other, as we had always assumed before this section.

The memory model changes made in Java 1.5 also extended the semantics of volatile variables. Writing or reading such a variable is now similar to acquiring or releasing a lock on the same object: accesses to volatile variables impose ordered memory barriers (point 3 above). Since code cannot be reordered across barriers (point 2), it means that accesses to non-volatile variables cannot be reordered with respect to accesses to volatile variables. Values visible to thread *A* when it writes to a volatile variable are also visible to thread *B* when it later reads the *same* volatile variable. Given that volatile variables are mostly used to signal changed conditions to threads, the new semantics ensures that a signalled thread is aware of updated values. Here is an example adapted from Manson and Goetz's *JSR 133 (Java Memory Model) FAQ* (2004).

```
class VolatileExample
{
    private int x = 0;
    private volatile boolean v = false;

    public void writer()
    {
        x = 42;
        v = true;
    }

    public void reader()
    {
        if (v == true)
        {
            System.out.println(x);
        }
    }
}
```

The implicit intention of the example is for the thread executing `writer` to inform the thread executing `reader` that the value of `x` has been updated, without having to use synchronisation.

With the pre-Java 1.5 memory model, all that was guaranteed was that any read access to `v` would always return the most recently written value. However, other than this there was nothing special about a volatile variable and therefore code could be reordered as usual. In the example, a possible execution sequence would be: one thread writes `v`, the other thread executes the `if` statement and prints out `0`, and the first thread finally updates `x`. With the memory model used from Java 1.5, any read or write access to `v` is a memory barrier and thus the assignments in `writer` cannot be reordered. The reading thread will print out the updated value, as intended.

SAQ 2

Why is the new semantics of volatile variables an *extension* of the old one?

ANSWER...

Because a memory barrier on each volatile variable access still forces the variable to be read from or written to shared memory, as required by the old memory model.

With the new memory model, volatile variables become more useful. They can make synchronisation unnecessary in some cases, leading to more efficient programs because lock acquisition and release not only has an overhead in itself, it also limits the amount of concurrency.

SAQ 3

Summarise the main points of this subsection by indicating:

(a) one of the central concerns for correctness of multithreaded applications;

(b) two problems that affect the achievement of correctness;

(c) the generic techniques that address the two problems specified in part (b);

(d) the concrete Java mechanisms that implement those techniques;

(e) how the mechanisms in part (d) can be used.

ANSWER..

(a) For a multithreaded application to behave correctly, changes made to shared variables by one thread must be visible to all other threads reading those variables.

(b) Updates in one thread might not be visible to other threads due to code reordering or because the values' copies held in local and shared memories are inconsistent.

(c) Mutual exclusion serialises accesses and this prevents the side effects of code reordering. To address the inconsistency problem, a memory model defines how value updates are propagated via memory barriers.

(d) Mutual exclusion is imposed by synchronised code. Memory barriers that make the values held locally by the thread consistent with those held in shared memory are created by accessing volatile variables or by synchronising code.

(e) Correct behaviour can be guaranteed only if threads synchronise on the *same* monitor or access the *same* volatile variable. Code is not reordered across memory barriers, which makes it possible to use volatile variables to flag changes to shared variables.

Before moving on to another topic, it is worth emphasising that the effects of code reordering and lack of memory barriers depend on the exact order and timing of the low-level machine code instructions and so can only rarely be observed. They are therefore seldom reproducible (i.e. only one particular execution of the program might have been incorrect) and hence very hard to detect during testing. The error might occur only when the system is in production, possibly with serious consequences, and such errors are always very difficult to trace back to their causes. It is therefore important to impose mutual exclusion and memory barriers whenever there is shared data. We will come back to this advice in Subsection 4.1.

2.4 | Threading models

JVM implementers not only have some freedom in how they translate the bytecode and memory areas to the platform's machine code and memory architecture, they can also choose how to implement threads: either to use **green threads** which are created, scheduled and terminated by the JVM itself, or to use **native threads** which are managed by the operating system. Using green threads makes the JVM implementation more complex, while using native threads delegates the burden of the work to the operating system.

Using green threads may be the best option if the underlying operating system supports processes only (and not threads), as, in that case, using native 'threads' would require the mapping of each Java thread to an operating system process. This may entail a performance penalty: having one process per Java thread and having to switch constantly between them is likely to consume more memory and CPU resources than having a single JVM process that manages its own threads internally.

However, it is more likely for JVM implementations to use native threads. First, because many current operating systems support threads; secondly, because using native threads simplifies the JVM implementation; and thirdly, because native threads can exploit the potential parallelism of the hardware. From the operating system perspective, with green Java threads there is a single JVM process to be scheduled to any of the available processors, regardless of the actual number of CPUs. Hence all Java threads will run on the same CPU, possibly leaving other CPUs idle. If native threads are used, then the operating system is aware of each Java thread and can schedule any runnable thread to any CPU. This makes better use of the machine's resources and will lead to better execution performance of the Java application.

Using native threads has the drawback that although Java provides its own threading model, the execution of a program will depend on the platform's threading model. As we have seen in *Unit 2*, the two major multitasking models are cooperative and pre-emptive. The cooperative model is very efficient, and the programmer does not have to worry about synchronisation, but must release resources at appropriate times to avoid starvation of other threads and to keep the system responsive. In pre-emptive models, the operating system does the scheduling, which entails an overhead, and the programmer has to worry about the atomicity of operations on shared data, but there is less risk of starvation.

Threading in Solaris.

The Solaris threading model

Most of the current operating system versions use pre-emptive multitasking, but, for example, early versions of the Microsoft Windows and Apple Macintosh operating systems used cooperative multitasking. Solaris, a Unix-based operating system developed by Sun Microsystems, has a bit of both models. In Solaris there are *user-level threads* which are initiated and terminated by the application, and there are *kernel threads* which are totally under the control of the operating system, in particular the scheduling of kernel threads on CPUs. The user-level threads correspond to Java threads, if the native thread approach is used (although this was not the case in Java 1.1). Each kernel thread executes a so-called *lightweight process* (LWP) in pre-emptive mode, and each LWP executes one or more user-level threads in a cooperative way. There may be a many-to-many mapping between user-level threads and LWPs or there might be a one-to-one mapping, and for each mapping there are further sub-options. All these possibilities have an effect on the execution performance or the behaviour of the application. For example, if each LWP runs only a single thread, there is no cooperative multitasking among user threads. To make it even more complex, which options are available and which one is used by default depends on the exact versions of the JVM and Solaris being used.

The example described in the box illustrates that the dependence of a JVM implementation on the operating system's threading model imposes contradictory pressures on the Java developer aiming for full platform independence: on the one hand, threads can be pre-empted anytime, and therefore attention must be paid to the need for mutual exclusion; on the other hand, threads may never be pre-empted, leading to a requirement that they periodically release control.

SAQ 4

Through which method calls can a Java thread release control?

ANSWER..

By calling `sleep`, `yield`, `wait` or `join` (*Unit 2*, Section 7).

When control passes to another thread, and there is a choice of which thread to schedule, usually the one with the highest priority will run. As we have seen in *Unit 2*, Section 7, Java threads can be assigned a priority from 1 (lowest) to 10 (highest). However, the JVM specification does not define any mapping to the particular operating system priorities. For example, Windows NT, an earlier version of the Windows operating system on which Windows XP was built, has less than 10 priority levels, which means that multiple Java priority levels have to be mapped to the same Windows NT priority level. Moreover, Windows NT has an automatic priority boosting mechanism for threads dealing with user interface operations to keep their responsiveness. The exact priority level of a thread is hence unknown beforehand and can change over time. For example, suppose that three Java threads with priorities 4, 5 and 6 are runnable, with the thread with priority 5 currently running. If that thread calls `yield`, the next thread to run is not necessarily the one with priority 6. Either thread can run if those three Java priority levels are mapped to the same Windows NT priority level. Even if they are mapped to different levels, the thread with Java priority 4 can run next if its Windows NT priority was boosted due to being previously blocked on an I/O operation.

The moral of the story is simple: it's best not to use priorities to control the execution order of threads, unless your program is going to run on a known fixed JVM, on a known fixed operating system for which you know how the Java priorities are mapped to the operating system priorities. Methods like `setPriority` and `yield` are merely suggestions to the JVM; each implementation is free to handle those methods as they wish. Such methods may be used to improve performance on a particular platform but programs should not depend on them for correctness. For special cases such as real-time systems that depend on reliable priority mechanisms, it is best to use special-purpose virtual machines and libraries that are beyond the scope of this course.

SAQ 5

Summarise the main points of this subsection by indicating:

(a) the two ways of implementing Java threads;

(b) the corresponding advantages and disadvantages;

(c) the consequences for writing platform-independent programs.

ANSWER...

(a) Among the decisions left open by the JVM specification is how to implement Java threads: they may be green threads, i.e. managed by the JVM, or native threads, i.e. managed by the operating system.

(b) Using green threads may be the best option if the underlying platform does not have threads, but the disadvantage is that the JVM implementation becomes more complex. Using native threads has the advantage of exploiting better the underlying platform resources, in particular if it has multiple processors. On the other hand, native threads make the behaviour of the Java program dependent on the way the operating system schedules and prioritises threads.

(c) This means that for a program to be truly platform independent it should:

    ▶ not use thread priorities;

    ▶ release control – via `wait` and `sleep` rather than `yield` – whenever adequate, to avoid problems if executed on a cooperative multitasking platform;

    ▶ access shared data only under mutual exclusion, so as to avoid problems if executed on a pre-emptive multitasking platform.

3 Concurrency utilities

In the previous sections we discussed the primitive concurrency constructs provided by the Java language (`synchronized`, `volatile`, `wait`), and the subtle problems that can arise when they are not used or are incorrectly used. But even if we apply the advice of the previous section, writing sophisticated and efficient concurrent programs can be laborious and cumbersome: laborious because any higher-level concurrency abstraction (e.g. semaphores) has to be implemented from scratch, and cumbersome because the built-in mechanisms have their limitations and require workarounds for specialised needs. In the remainder of this unit we explore those limitations and take a look at the concurrency utilities introduced with Java 1.5: they ease the development of concurrent programs by introducing higher-level concurrency abstractions and by overcoming some of the built-in limitations.

3.1 Java's limitations

Java's built-in support for concurrency has its strengths but also its limitations. On the one hand, the concurrency model is simple and integrated into the language, which makes life easier for programmers, e.g. locks are automatically released. On the other hand, Java's basic mechanisms are not flexible or expressive enough for complex concurrent applications. Several shortcomings have been noted by developers, including the following.

▶ Java monitors do not exactly correspond to the generic monitor concept. In particular, Java monitors have a single anonymous condition variable instead of an explicit set of condition variables, as we have noted in *Unit 3*, Section 4. This makes it impossible to distinguish threads that are waiting for the same lock but on different conditions. Such a distinction could make programs more efficient because it would not be necessary to notify all threads indiscriminately. Explicit distinct condition variables also make programs easier to understand and hence maintain.

▶ A thread can state for how long it is willing to wait for a notification, but it cannot state for how long it is willing to block when waiting for the lock to become available: once a thread attempts to acquire a lock, there is no 'backtracking' and the thread may be blocked indefinitely if there is a deadlock. To help avoid such situations, it would be useful to have a kind of 'timed blocking', akin to timed waiting (*Unit 2*, Section 7).

▶ As we have seen in Subsection 2.4, Java provides poor support for priorities: they mostly depend on the underlying operating system threading model. The application cannot assume that the runnable thread with highest Java priority will be the one scheduled to run next. However, real-time systems need such guarantees and therefore they need an accurate and reliable priority model. We will not pursue this issue further, as real-time systems are outside the scope of this course.

To overcome some of these shortcomings, Java 1.5 introduced a new package of concurrency utilities, `java.util.concurrent`, based on the package described by Lea (1999). The new package was developed following the Java Community Process, in reply to the Java Specification Request 166. This means that the development of these utilities had feedback from Java developers, to ensure their needs are met. Using such a package has the following advantages over developing your own routines and data abstractions:

The Java Community Process.

▶ productivity increases because you can use and extend off-the-shelf classes instead of reinventing the wheel;

▶ maintenance is facilitated because the utilities are part of a standard library supported by Sun Microsystems;

▶ performance and reliability are improved because the library was developed by concurrency experts.

To summarise, the concurrency utilities include:

▶ new collections that perform better and more flexibly under concurrent access;

▶ variables that can be compared and set atomically in an efficient lock-free way (i.e. threads do not have to block) on many platforms, thereby improving the performance of concurrent applications;

▶ lock objects with, among other features, multiple condition variables and timeouts, thereby addressing some of the above-mentioned limitations;

▶ several general-purpose high-level abstractions, including semaphores, in order to coordinate threads in an easier way;

▶ a general framework for scheduling asynchronous tasks in an efficient way.

We will now introduce you to some of the available library classes and their functionality, but a comprehensive treatment of Java's concurrency utilities is outside the aims of this course.

3.2 | Concurrent collections

The Java Collections Framework has been greatly changed and enhanced in Java 1.5, but we will focus only on issues related to concurrency and we will concentrate only on one kind of collection – lists – because they illustrate the main points that also apply to other interfaces and classes in the framework. First we will briefly recap the operations provided on lists and the list implementations included in the Java libraries.

Lists

The Java Collections Framework consists of interfaces that define commonly used abstract data types, such as lists and sets, together with classes that implement those data structures in various ways.

The `java.util.Collection` interface declares the operations common to all collections. Since Java 1.5, it has been possible to constrain the types of element within a collection. For example, `Collection<Integer> elements;` states that all elements are integer objects. The declaration `Collection elements;` is equivalent to `Collection<Object> elements;` and allows each element to be any object.

A list is an ordered collection of elements, allowing for duplicates; by contrast, sets are unordered collections of unique elements. Being an ordered collection means that each element has a unique position within the collection. Positions are numbered from 0 onwards. The head of a list is the element at position 0, the tail of the list is the element in the last position. The `java.util.List` interface extends the `Collection` interface and provides operations to insert, remove and search for elements in a list. Some of the most useful operations are listed in Table 2.

Table 2 Some methods of the `List` interface

Method	Description
`void add(int index, Object o)`	Inserts the element at the given position.
`boolean add(Object o)`	Appends the element to the tail of the list, returning `true`.
`int indexOf(Object o)`	Returns the position of the first occurrence of the element, or `-1` if it does not exist.
`Object get(int index)`	Returns the element at the given position.
`Object remove(int index)`	Removes the element at the given position.
`boolean remove(Object o)`	Removes the first occurrence of the given element, returning `false` if the element does not exist in the list.
`int size()`	Returns the number of elements in the list.

If `index` is negative or larger than the list's size, the corresponding methods return `IndexOutOfBoundsException`.

The generic way of visiting all the elements of a collection is to create an iterator. The following two examples show the typical iteration idiom. The first method prints out all the elements in a list; the second removes all elements that do not satisfy some condition which is tested by a method called `cond`.

```
public void print (Collection c)
{
   for (Iterator i = c.iterator(); i.hasNext(); )
   {
      System.out.println(i.next().toString());
   }
}

public void filter (Collection c)
{
   for (Iterator i = c.iterator(); i.hasNext(); )
   {
      if (! cond(i.next()))
      {
         i.remove();
      }
   }
}
```

The `iterator` method is supported by all collections and creates the iterator. Method `hasNext` returns `true` if there is still an unvisited element, and `next` returns an unvisited element. The method `remove` is optional, i.e. it may not be implemented by all iterators. It deletes from the collection the element last visited, which means that `remove` can only be called after `next`. Finally, note that instead of using `for` loops you can write:

```
Iterator i = c.iterator();
while (i.hasNext())
{
   // do something with i.next()
}
```

Since the release of Java 1.5, *for-each* loops may be used instead of iterators, to go through a collection:

```
Collection c = ...;
for (Object o : c)
{
   // do something with o
}
```

However, if you wish to delete some elements as you traverse the collection, you must use an iterator and call its `remove` method.

An abstract data type can be implemented in various ways, each implementation making some operations more efficient than others. The programmer will have to choose the implementation that favours those operations most frequently used in the application at hand. In the case of lists, the two most common ways of implementing them are using arrays or linked lists. In a linked list, each item in the list has two parts: the list element and a reference to the next item (or the `null` reference if it is the last item).

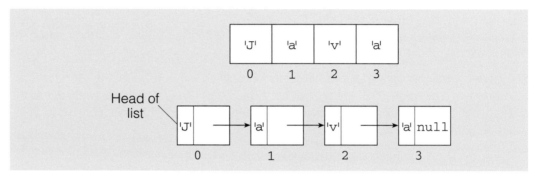

Figure 2   Two implementations of a list with four character elements: an array and a linked list

Retrieving an element by position (using the `get` method of Table 2) is much more efficient with an array than with a linked list, because arrays allow direct indexing of any element, whereas in linked lists all the elements up to the given position have to be traversed one by one. On the other hand, the `add` and `remove` methods can be implemented more efficiently with a linked list, because it amounts to changing a few references, whereas in an array all elements after the inserted or deleted element have to be shifted up or down.

In the Java Collections Framework, classes `ArrayList` and `LinkedList` implement `List` in the way their names imply. However, the first array-based implementation of lists was the class `Vector`, available since Java 1.0. The Collections Framework was introduced in Java 1.2, and `Vector` was 'reprogrammed' in order to comply with the `List` interface. The reason why a second array-based implementation, class `ArrayList`, was added, was due to concurrency issues.

Concurrency issues

At the time of Java 1.2, synchronisation was not as efficient as it is today. Therefore, single-threaded applications using synchronised collections (`Vector` being one of them) incurred a performance penalty imposed by a feature they did not need. The Java Collections Framework created in Java 1.2 therefore introduced unsynchronised classes, including `ArrayList` and `LinkedList`.

However, multithreaded applications still need synchronised collections. The synchronised 'version' of `ArrayList` already existed, namely class `Vector`, but there was no such counterpart for other classes like `LinkedList`. Instead of creating two versions of each new class in the Collections Framework, the Java designers decided to introduce in Java 1.2 a utility class `Collections` (note the plural!) with static methods that create synchronised versions of unsynchronised classes. For lists, the method is `synchronizedList(List list)`, which returns a list object with the same content as `list` but guaranteeing atomic execution of each operation. Methods like this one are called **wrapper methods** because they wrap new functionality (in this case, synchronisation) around existing objects.

While synchronising each method guarantees that every *single* read/write access to the collection is well behaved, it does not guarantee that a *sequence* of accesses will execute correctly. For example, it is possible for one thread to modify a collection while another is iterating over it, and this can lead to problems. Consider the following simple scenario. A thread starts iterating over a collection with a single element. The thread calls `hasNext`, which returns `true`. At this point the thread is pre-empted by another one that removes the element from the list. The first thread resumes execution and calls `next`, but the element no longer exists and `NoSuchElementException` is thrown.

More subtle problems can occur if the iterator is allowed to view the collection in an inconsistent state because another thread is concurrently adding, removing or changing elements. To avoid such hard to debug problems, the iterators are **fail-fast**: they stop as soon as they detect that some other thread is modifying the collection and throw the `ConcurrentModificationException`.

The best and simplest way to avoid problems is, of course, to lock the collection while it is traversed. Here is an example of how to create a synchronised linked list and iterate over it.

```
List aList = Collections.synchronizedList(new LinkedList());

synchronize(aList)
{
  for (Iterator i = aList.iterator(); i.hasNext(); )
  {
    // do something with i.next()
  }
}
```

Note that although by construction each *single* access to `aList` is synchronised, that is not enough to guarantee mutual exclusion to the *whole* collection during iteration. Hence, the code using the list has to acquire a lock on it. This is an example where both the class and the code that uses the class have to provide synchronisation. We will return in Subsection 4.5 to the issue of the 'amount' of synchronisation needed.

The problem with the above solution is that it prevents multiple concurrent read accesses to the same collection, which reduces the performance of the application. To overcome this problem, Java 1.5 introduced new classes that provide better concurrency support for collections.

Concurrency support

Whereas the collection interfaces and classes mentioned so far are in the `java.util` package, the 'concurrent collections' are in `java.util.concurrent`. They are, in general, synchronised, and iterators created by them are **weakly consistent**. This means that the *view* of the collection provided by the iterator is not necessarily consistent with the current content of the collection. The advantage of requiring less from iterators is that they never fail.

For example, one of the new classes is `CopyOnWriteArrayList`, a synchronised version of `ArrayList` with a weakly consistent iterator. As the name of the class implies, whenever the list is about to change, a fresh copy of the underlying array is made and the change is done on the new copy. Whenever an iterator is created, it will traverse the current copy of the array. Since any further modifications are done on new copies, the iterator will not be aware of them and therefore does not raise an exception. In other words, the iterator provides a view of the collection as it was when the iterator was created, but the collection may have changed in the meantime.

Copying the underlying array each time it is changed entails a performance penalty, but it may be worthwhile if traversals (read operations) significantly outnumber modifications (write operations). In that case, multiple threads can concurrently read the collection, which is not possible with `ArrayList`, and the overall execution time may in fact be reduced, in spite of the occasional copy operations when the collection is modified.

Besides changing the semantics of iterators slightly in order to improve concurrent access, in Java 1.5 the Collections Framework introduced the `java.util.Queue` interface. It is a much simpler interface than `List`, and should be used when the full flexibility of retrieving, adding and removing elements from any position in the list is not needed. Elements in a queue are always removed from the head, but various policies are possible as to where they are inserted, depending on the implementation of the interface. Typically, elements are inserted at the tail, leading to a FIFO (first-in, first-out) policy. But in a **priority queue**, the position where an element is inserted depends on the priority that has been associated with the element. In this way, the next element to be removed from the queue is guaranteed to be the one with the currently highest priority.

SAQ 6

Can you recall, from earlier in the course, a context where priority queues might be useful?

ANSWER...

Priority queues are useful when implementing process schedulers (*Unit 2*, Section 5). Each element in the queue consists of a pair of numbers – the unique process ID and the process priority. The next process to be scheduled is the one at the front of the priority queue.

Note the different packages that `Queue` and `BlockingQueue` are part of.

The `java.util.Queue` interface is extended by the interface `java.util.concurrent.BlockingQueue`, which adds the following methods.

```
public void put(Object o)
public Object take()
```

The two methods insert and remove an element from the queue, but force a thread to wait if the operation is not possible, instead of raising an exception. For example, if a thread is trying to remove an element from an empty queue, it will wait until the queue is non-empty. Similarly, a thread attempting to put an element into a full queue will wait for it to become non-full.

Exercise 9

Sketch the implementation of `take` and `put`, based on the above description.

Discussion...

The main point is for the methods to wait while the queue is empty or full, and to notify any other thread waiting on the same queue that the queue has changed so that the condition for putting or taking an element can be rechecked.

```
public synchronized Object take()
{
  Object o;

  while (/*this queue is empty*/)
  {
    wait();
  }
  // remove first element from queue and store it in o
  notifyAll();
  return o;
}

public synchronized void put(Object o)
{
  while (/*this queue is full*/)
  {
    wait();
  }
  // put o at the end of the queue
  notifyAll();
}
```

Queues are often used in producer–consumer settings (*Unit 3*, Section 2). A blocking queue that is bounded, i.e. has a maximum size, is an elegant way of avoiding excessive use of resources and degradation of performance. If producers are generating elements much faster than consumers are using them, an unbounded non-blocking queue will continuously grow, whereas a bounded blocking queue will force producers to wait: memory usage is kept constant, the number of runnable threads is diminished, and throughput (number of consumed elements per time unit) grows.

The use of blocking queues raises one question: how do you prevent a consumer thread from waiting indefinitely on an element that will never be put into the empty queue? The usual way is to have some agreed special 'end-of-stream' element that signals that no further elements will be put into the queue.

The Collections Framework provides various implementations of the `BlockingQueue` interface in order to cater for different needs. For example, `ArrayBlockingQueue` is a bounded FIFO queue, while `PriorityBlockingQueue` is an unbounded priority queue. There are various other implementations, but we will not go into further details.

3.3 Atomic variables

In *Unit 3*, Section 3, we saw that an atomic test-and-set (TAS) operation is useful to implement mutual exclusion algorithms. Such an operation can be simulated with a synchronised block of code, for example:

```
Boolean b;
...
synchronized (b)
{
  if (b.equals (Boolean.TRUE)) b = Boolean.FALSE;
}
```

Note that we have to use the `Boolean` class instead of the `boolean` primitive type, because synchronisation works only on objects, not on primitive data that lacks internal monitors.

However, as said in *Unit 3*, many CPUs have a TAS machine code instruction. Using such an instruction, instead of having to obtain a lock, would make concurrent Java programs faster.

One of the aims of package `java.util.concurrent.atomic` is to provide such TAS operations for several types of value. In particular, the package includes classes like `AtomicInteger` and `AtomicBoolean` that implement a `compareAndSet` method. The above example would be simply written as

```
AtomicBoolean b;
...
b.compareAndSet(true, false);
```

Simply put, atomic variables can be seen as volatile variables on which all methods execute atomically. For example, class `AtomicInteger` provides the method `getAndIncrement` which returns the current variable's value and then increments it. Compare the following examples.

Example 1

```
public class Counter
{
    private int i = 1;

    public synchronized int next()
    {
      return i++;
    }
}
```

Example 2

```
import java.util.concurrent.atomic.AtomicInteger;
public class Counter
{
    private AtomicInteger i = new AtomicInteger(1);

    public int next()
    {
      return i.getAndIncrement();
    }
}
```

Whereas the expression `i++` in the first example is a sequence of operations to read the value, increment it and store it in the variable, the expression `i.getAndIncrement()` in the second example is a single operation. Atomic variables thus make it possible to write thread-safe counters without using synchronised code. Multiple threads can call `next` concurrently with the guarantee that they will obtain consecutive values for the counter. Essentially, atomic variables behave like volatile variables in that they always read and write from shared memory. Therefore, any increment due to a thread calling `next` will be visible to the next thread calling the method.

Although it is possible to obtain the same effect as atomic variables by putting variable accesses – like the `if` statement and the `i++` expression – within synchronised code, the whole point of using atomic variables is that concrete implementations are likely to use the hardware's low-level TAS instructions. If the hardware does not provide such atomic operations, then the implementation uses synchronisation to achieve thread safety.

This means that on many hardware platforms, atomic variables are lock free and hence provide better **scalability under contention** than using normal variables with synchronised methods. Scalability under contention is the capacity to maintain a high throughput (in this case, the number of read/write accesses to a variable) when multiple threads are trying to use the same resource (in this case, an atomic variable). In a lock-free scenario, threads do not block because by definition there is no lock to be acquired. If threads do not block, then less time is spent by the JVM in scheduling threads, leaving more time to actually execute them. Atomic variables can therefore not only make the code simpler, but also make it run faster. It is therefore no surprise that a large part of the concurrency utilities package is implemented using atomic variables.

3.4 | Locks

To overcome some of the limitations mentioned in Subsection 3.1, the package `java.util.concurrent.locks` was introduced in Java 1.5. It includes two interfaces `Lock` and `Condition` which generalise the lock and the single implicit condition variable of Java's built-in monitors. The interfaces allow a more conventional style of concurrency programming, in which the application's objects, the locks and the condition variables are three separate entities.

The `Lock` interface

Locks have to be explicitly acquired and released by calling `lock` and `unlock` methods. This has a big disadvantage: if the developer forgets to call `unlock`, the application might deadlock. Such a situation cannot happen with the built-in object locks because they are automatically released by the JVM when the synchronised code finishes, even if it is abruptly terminated due to an exception.

Consider the following.

```
try
{
  synchronized (myObject)
  {
    // operations to be done under mutual exclusion
  }
}
catch (Exception e)
{
  // deal with exception
}
```

The corresponding usage pattern with `Lock` objects should be as follows.

```
Lock myLock;
...
myLock.lock();
try
{
   // operations to be done under mutual exclusion
}
catch (Exception e)
{
   // deal with exception
}
finally
{
   myLock.unlock();
}
```

The `Lock` interface also includes two `boolean` methods to try to acquire a lock without blocking if the lock is not available:

`tryLock()` returns `false` if the lock is unavailable, otherwise acquires it and returns `true`;

`tryLock(long time, TimeUnit unit)` tries to acquire the lock within the given time, returning `true` or `false` to signal success or failure.

For example, `myLock.tryLock(3400, TimeUnit.MILLISECONDS)` will block the thread for up to 3.4 seconds in order to try and acquire the lock `myLock`. A typical usage pattern is:

```
if (myLock.tryLock())
{
   try
   {
      // operations to be done under mutual exclusion
   }
   catch (Exception e)
   {
      // deal with exception
   }
   finally
   {
      myLock.unlock();
   }
}
else
{
   // alternative actions if lock is unavailable
}
```

Although developers may provide their own implementations of the `Lock` interface, the concurrency utilities already include one, the `ReentrantLock` class, so named because it provides a re-entrant lock, like Java's built-in monitor locks.

SAQ 7

What is a re-entrant lock?

ANSWER...

A re-entrant lock can be reacquired by a thread that already holds it (*Unit 3*, Section 4).

Class `ReentrantLock` is implemented in terms of atomic variables. It therefore has better performance and scales better under contention than synchronised objects, provided that the platform running the application has built-in low-level atomic operations. However, keep in mind that synchronisation is often uncontended (that is, only one thread is trying to acquire the lock), in which case it has a low performance penalty on many platforms. The performance gain of using `ReentrantLock` might therefore be smaller than expected.

The `Condition` interface

As mentioned before, the `java.util.concurrent.locks` package also provides an interface `Condition` to allow *multiple explicit* condition variables for each lock. We first look at the problems of Java's built-in *single anonymous* condition variable, by revisiting the code we used in the discussion of Exercise 9:

```
public synchronized Object take()
{
  Object o;

  while (/*this queue is empty*/)
  {
    wait();
  }
  // remove first element from queue and store it in o
  notifyAll();
  return o;
}

public synchronized void put(Object o)
{
  while (/*this queue is full*/)
  {
    wait();
  }
  // put o at the end of the queue
  notifyAll();
}
```

The above methods use Java's built-in monitors with a single anonymous condition variable. That makes it impossible to distinguish which threads are waiting for the queue to become non empty, so that they can `take` an element, and which ones are waiting for it to become non-full, so that they can `put` an element. Therefore *all* threads have to be notified on *any* change to the queue. There will be contention to reacquire the lock, and some threads are likely to have to wait again: they obtain the lock but find the condition to be still false.

Now let us see how the `Condition` interface can help us improve the above code. A condition variable is created by calling `newCondition()` on the `Lock` object. Some of the methods provided by the interface are:

```
void await()
boolean await(long time, TimeUnit unit)
void signal()
void signalAll()
```

These methods are the counterpart of the `Object` methods `wait()`, `wait(time)` with `time` being in milliseconds, `notify()` and `notifyAll()`. For example, when a thread calls `c.await()`, it will be added to the wait set of condition variable `c`; and when a thread calls `c.signal()`, one other thread waiting on condition `c` is notified. As an example of condition variables, we will provide an improved implementation of the BlockingQueue.

With explicit condition variables, we can have one for the condition 'the queue is not full' and another for 'the queue is not empty'. Threads attempting to put an element must wait on the first condition to become true; threads attempting to take an element must wait on the second to become true. Dividing the threads into two wait sets means that only *one* thread has to be notified: whenever one element is put, one of the threads attempting a take is notified, and vice versa. The queue hence becomes more scalable under contention, because less time is spent in notifying and putting on wait again the 'wrong' threads.

```java
public class MyBlockingQueue implements BlockingQueue
{
  private Lock lock = new ReentrantLock();
  private Condition notFull = lock.newCondition();
  private Condition notEmpty = lock.newCondition();

  public void put(Object x) throws InterruptedException
  {
    lock.lock();
    try
    {
      while (/*queue is full*/)
      {
        notFull.await();
      }
      // put x into queue
      notEmpty.signal();
    }
    finally
    {
      lock.unlock();
    }
  }

  public Object take() throws InterruptedException
  {
    lock.lock();
    try
    {
      while (/*queue is empty*/)
      {
        notEmpty.await();
      }
      // take an element from the queue
      notFull.signal();
      // return the element;
    }
    finally
    {
      lock.unlock();
    }
  }
}
```

Note that the code uses a `try-finally` statement to guarantee the release of the lock in all cases, and that the waits are within loops that test for the negation of the condition that will be waited for.

Java's built-in monitors throw `IllegalMonitorStateException` if the thread attempts to wait on, or notify, a monitor for which it does not hold the lock. The `Condition` interface does not impose such behaviour, but the condition variables created by `ReentrantLock` do mimic the normal monitor behaviour.

SAQ 8

List some shortcomings of Java's built-in monitors and how they are addressed by the interfaces and classes of the `java.util.concurrent.locks` package.

ANSWER...

Some disadvantages of the built-in monitors are:

▶ no separation of data, lock, and condition variables;

▶ one single condition variable per lock;

▶ an attempt to acquire a lock cannot be cancelled.

The `Lock` and `Condition` interfaces allow the creation of explicit locks that are separate objects, and the creation of multiple conditions per lock. Moreover, the `Lock` interface allows a thread to timeout on acquiring a lock or to avoid blocking if the lock is not available.

3.5 Synchronisers

The concurrency utilities not only improve on the built-in mechanisms, such as volatile variables and monitors, they also provide higher-level abstractions that facilitate coordination among several threads.

Semaphores

Semaphores were discussed at length in *Unit 3*, Section 3. To recap, a counting semaphore holds a certain number of *permits*, and there are two operations to acquire or release one or more permits. If a thread tries to acquire more permits than are currently available, it will wait for the necessary number to become available. In effect, binary and blocking semaphores are just special cases of counting semaphores, with the number of permits initialised to 1 and 0, respectively.

Java 1.5 introduced the `java.util.concurrent.Semaphore` class which includes the constructor

```
Semaphore (int permits)
```

and the methods

```
void acquire(int permits)
void release(int permits)
boolean tryAcquire(int permits)
boolean tryAcquire(int permits, long timeout, TimeUnit unit)
```

As you can see, the API is very similar to `Lock`: it has an acquisition and a release method, a non-blocking acquisition method and a timed-out acquisition method. There are also versions without the permits number (defaulting to 1).

To illustrate the use of semaphores, we implement the car park example of *Unit 3*, Section 4, with two extensions: we allow multiple spaces to be taken up by a single vehicle (e.g. a coach might take up two spaces) and we allow a vehicle to indicate how many minutes it is willing to wait for available space if the car park is full. We also use the Semaphore method `availablePermits` to compute how many parking spaces are free.

```java
import java.util.concurrent.Semaphore;
import java.util.concurrent.TimeUnit;

public class CarPark
{
  private Semaphore available;

  CarPark(int spaces)
  {
    available = new Semaphore(spaces);
  }

  public boolean enter(int needed, int wait) throws InterruptedException
  {
    boolean result = available.tryAcquire(needed, wait*60,
      TimeUnit.SECONDS);
    System.out.println("Available spaces: "
      + available.availablePermits());
    return result;
  }

  public void exit(int used)
  {
    available.release(used);
    System.out.println("Available spaces: "
      + available.availablePermits());
  }
}
```

One of the distinctive characteristics of semaphores is that, contrary to locks, there is no notion of ownership, i.e. a semaphore does not keep track of which threads acquired which permits. In the above example, the CarPark class is relying on each thread to behave properly, i.e. to release as many parking spaces as they have acquired. Otherwise, the capacity of the car park will appear to shrink or grow.

Activity 4.2
Semaphore example.

The moral of the story is: if a class is using counting semaphores to acquire and release resources (e.g. parking spaces), then the class itself must manage the mapping of resources to permits if it cannot rely on well-behaved clients. However, managing resources under concurrent access requires synchronisation and semaphores become redundant. In a language like Java, which has built-in mutual exclusion mechanisms, semaphores are truly useful in only a few situations, e.g. for condition synchronisation (see 'Using semaphores for process synchronisation' in *Unit 3*, Section 3).

Countdown latches

One of the other coordination aids in the concurrency utilities is the CountDownLatch class. A **countdown latch** basically implements a thread execution barrier with a counter. If the counter is positive, the barrier is down and any thread arriving at the latch has to wait; if the counter is 0, the barrier is up and all waiting threads can resume execution. A simple analogy is a train crossing barrier, where each car is a thread and the number of trains approaching the barrier is the value of the counter. If one train is approaching (i.e. the counter is 1), the barrier is down and the cars have to wait. The train passing the barrier corresponds to decrementing the counter and hence the barrier goes up and the cars can proceed.

Figure 3   An analogy of a countdown latch

The latch has only two operations: a 'wait' operation that indicates that a thread has arrived at the barrier, and a 'notify' operation that decrements the counter. The counter is initialised to a given value when the latch is created, and the barrier will therefore go up only after the necessary number of notifications have been issued. Notice that there is no operation to increment the counter, i.e. once the barrier is up, it stays up – this is where the train crossing analogy breaks down. Threads arriving at a latch that is up will not have to wait and can proceed to execution immediately.

The concrete API is given in Table 3.

Table 3   CountDownLatch API

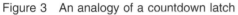

Method	Description
CountDownLatch(int count)	Constructor raises an exception if the parameter is negative.
void await()	Returns immediately if the counter is 0, otherwise puts the thread on wait until the counter becomes 0.
void countDown()	Decrements the counter.

To state it succinctly, a countdown latch allows one group of threads to wait until another group of threads has performed some operations. Each thread in the first group only calls the await method, while each thread in the second group calls countDown whenever it finishes doing its part of the operations. This makes a countdown latch a very flexible thread-coordination mechanism.

For example, consider a MUD (multi-user dungeon) game running on a server machine to which players connect from their home machines. The server application may have one thread per player to process his or her commands (move north, pick object, etc.) and one thread to set up the dungeon (put objects in different rooms, etc.). The player threads can start by initialising the player's characteristics, but they cannot start processing player commands until the dungeon thread has finished the set-up.

Exercise 10

If the MUD application is to use a countdown latch, which threads are waiting on the latch to go up, and which thread or threads raise the latch? What is the initial value of the counter?

Discussion..

The counter is initialised with a value of 1, the player threads wait on the latch, and the dungeon thread calls `countDown` once it has finished the set-up.

Note that if the dungeon thread is faster than a player thread, the latter will find the latch already up when calling `await` and therefore proceed without waiting. The whole point of latches is to guarantee that one group of threads can proceed only if another group of threads says it is safe to do so. It therefore does not matter what happens first, the first group arriving at the barrier or the second group giving the go-ahead. The latch will always impose the overall condition, whatever the individual execution speed of the individual threads.

Divide-and-conquer.

To further illustrate the flexibility of countdown latches, consider an application that has to compute the solution to a complex scientific problem by following a particular **divide-and-conquer** strategy of decomposing the problem into *N* independent subproblems and then combining the subsolutions together. The application can follow a **master–slave model**: there is one master thread that partitions the problem into subproblems, and there are *N* slave threads, each one solving one subproblem and generating one subsolution, which the master thread then combines into the overall solution. One advantage of this strategy is to exploit any potential parallelism in solving the subproblems.

Countdown latches are an easy way to coordinate the execution of the master and slave threads. The counter is initialised to *N*, and the master thread creates the slave threads and then waits on the latch. As for the slave threads, each one decrements the counter when it has solved its subproblem. In this way, when all slave threads finish, the counter reaches 0, and the main thread can proceed with the combination of the subsolutions.

Activity 4.3

Latch example.

Note how the two examples are 'symmetric'. In the MUD example, *N* threads wait on a single thread; in the divide-and-conquer example, one thread waits on *N* threads. The activity for this subsection provides a concrete program using latches.

3.6   Task scheduling

It is often the case that tasks to be executed (i.e. `Runnable` objects) are rather short-lived, for example when handling a user interface event or returning a web page to a client. It would be foolish to create a new thread to handle each such task, because thread creation and termination takes time, threads require extra memory (Subsection 2.2), and the more runnable threads there are, the more time is spent in scheduling instead of on task execution (we will return to this point in Subsection 4.4). In summary, performance can degrade substantially, depending on the number of tasks.

A better approach is to use a dedicated task execution service where tasks are queued and a **thread pool** handles them. Each thread in the pool takes one task from the queue, executes it, and then goes back to the queue to fetch another task, if there is one. This makes better use of resources, because threads are being reused by multiple tasks, thus reducing the overhead involved in thread creation, termination and scheduling.

Using a thread pool is often quite simple: there is one operation to put a task in the queue, and another to close the service so that no further tasks can be submitted. The main problem is to set up the service properly so that effective resource management and good performance are achieved. Creating the service involves making the following decisions, among others.

▶ Should the pool be bounded or unbounded? In an unbounded pool, a new thread will be created whenever needed, while in a bounded pool there is a maximum number of threads. If all the threads are busy, a task will have to wait for a thread to finish processing its current task. A bounded pool imposes a limit on the overall use of resources but may reduce throughput.

▶ Should the queue be bounded or unbounded? With an unbounded queue, tasks can always be submitted for execution. If the queue is bounded, only a certain number of tasks can wait for threads to become available.

▶ If the queue is bounded, what should happen if a task is submitted when the queue is full? Various policies are possible, including: the task is ignored; the task is rejected and an exception is raised; the longest waiting task in the queue is removed to give place to the new task; or the thread submitting the task has to execute it.

▶ If threads in the pool are idle for some time, they could be removed to save resources, but what timing threshold should be set for threads to be terminated?

Some of these decisions impact on the behaviour of the system, while others impact on the throughput of the system. The former types of decision should be taken when the system is developed, with the latter being taken after testing the system under production conditions. For example, the policy on what to do if the queue is full affects how the application is programmed, but the pool size should have no bearing on the correctness of the application. The optimal size will have to be determined by running the application with different values and seeing which one leads to the best performance. If the pool size is too large for the needs of the application, many idle threads will waste resources; if the pool size is too small, many tasks will have to spend time waiting.

The concurrency utilities which support task scheduling include an interface ExecutorService with the following methods, among others.

```
void execute(Runnable r)
void shutdown()
```

The first method submits task r to the execution service. If the task is rejected, a RejectedExecutionException is raised. Otherwise r.run() will eventually be called. The shutdown method properly terminates the execution service. This will reject any further task submissions and allow the current tasks to finish, after which the service is terminated.

Class ThreadPoolExecutor is a very flexible implementation of ExecutorService. The class has various constructors and methods to set the pool size, the maximal idle time, the kind of queue to use, the method to be called after a task terminates (e.g. for logging purposes), etc. We will not go into the quite complex details of this class.

Instead, we will take a much easier way to create thread pools, by calling **factory methods** of the Executors class. A factory method is a method that creates objects of a given type C. Typically, factory methods are static methods and C is an interface. They are used when either the creation of a C object is complex, or the exact implementation of C should be kept hidden. In our case, creating a thread pool may require complex parameterisation of ThreadPoolExecutor, or may require a different implementation of the ExecutorService interface. Factory methods are therefore ideally suited to creating commonly used thread pools. Two examples are:

▶ static ExecutorService newCachedThreadPool() returns a service, with an unlimited pool, that creates a new thread whenever no thread is available to execute the task, and removes threads that are idle for 1 minute;

▶   `static ExecutorService newFixedThreadPool(int n)` returns a service with an unbounded queue and a pool with n threads.

A pool with one thread (i.e. n has the value 1) is useful if executing multiple tasks concurrently may lead to very complex and possibly erroneous behaviour. An example is the single GUI event-handling thread (*Unit 2*, Section 7).

Exercise 11

At the start of this subsection we said that creating a new thread for each task is usually a waste of resources. But the `newCachedThreadPool` seems to do exactly that. What is the difference?

Discussion...

A thread pool *reuses* available threads, i.e. the cached thread pool only creates a new thread if no other thread can immediately execute the submitted task. In the best case, a cached thread pool will use only one thread if each task completes before the next one is submitted. Moreover, a cached thread pool also automatically terminates unused threads.

Activity 4.4

Executor example.

The activity for this subsection shows you how to use cached and fixed-size thread pools and allows you to compare their behaviour. However, keep in mind that to obtain the best possible performance, you should use the more flexible classes provided by the concurrency utilities, of which `ThreadPoolExecutor` is one, and then fine-tune the settings during system testing.

4 Thread safety

After the discussion of generic concurrency problems in *Unit 3* and the specific JVM pitfalls in this unit, you could be forgiven for thinking that writing concurrent programs is incredibly difficult and that it is almost impossible to get any concurrent program working on one platform, let alone on multiple platforms. You may find some consolation in knowing that even professional experts do not always get it right: Sun Microsystems' JVM for Java 1.5 fixed 8000 bugs, and some concurrency-related bugs have been found in previous versions of the Java API. But you may find these facts disturb your confidence even more: if even the experts have difficulties, what are the chances of 'normal' programmers building correct concurrent programs?

The reality is not so bleak. On the one hand, many applications are inherently concurrent, as mentioned in *Unit 1*. In those cases, writing a single-threaded Java program would actually be much more difficult because the resulting control flow would be a spaghetti-like mess executing each concurrent task a bit at a time to make sure the system is responsive to the users. This would almost amount to writing your own scheduler and the cooperative tasks, all rolled into a single thread. On the other hand, several of the problems in writing concurrent programs arise only when dealing with advanced concurrency features or when trying to be 'smart' by, for example, tweaking the thread priorities to force a particular execution order, or saving on synchronisation in the interest of performance. Do not forget Einstein's maxim 'everything should be made as simple as possible, but no simpler' and Knuth's dictum 'premature optimisation is the root of all evil' (McConnell, 2004, p. 594). These comments apply to software design and programming in general, including writing concurrent programs.

The remainder of this section, which is largely based on Bloch (2001, Chapter 9), gives you some generic advice on writing code that behaves correctly even if executed by multiple threads. Bloch's advice on staying clear of the many pitfalls of concurrent programming can be summarised as follows.

▶ Synchronise access to shared mutable data.

▶ Avoid unnecessary synchronisation.

▶ Always call `wait` inside a loop.

▶ Do not depend on the thread scheduler.

▶ Document thread safety.

We now look at each of these in more detail.

4.1 Synchronise access to shared mutable data

Whenever multiple threads share some mutable data, i.e. data that is changeable, the code that accesses such data should be synchronised. This important piece of advice will enable the developer to avoid many problems.

Exercise 12

In the `MyThread` example of Subsection 2.3, one thread reads the `boolean` variable `done` and another thread writes to it. The variable is therefore shared mutable data. Modify the code so that accesses to it are synchronised.

Discussion...

```
class MyThread extends Thread
{
  private boolean done = false;

  public void run()
  {
    while (! isDone())
    {
      // do something
      try
      {
        Thread.sleep(100);
      }
      catch(InterruptedException e)
      {
        // handle exception
      }
    }
  }

  public synchronized boolean isDone()
  {
    return done;
  }

  public synchronized void finish()
  {
    done = true;
  }
}
```

As we said in Subsection 2.3, synchronisation imposes mutual exclusion *and* memory barriers. The former prevents race conditions, the latter forces reliable communication of shared data among threads. Strictly speaking, in the discussion of Exercise 12 mutual exclusion is not needed because in Java a read or write access to a primitive value (except of type `long` or `double`) is an atomic operation. In other words, the mutual exclusion is already guaranteed by the type of data used.

However, we still need to add the memory barrier, so the class `MyThread` could also have been implemented by simply declaring the variable `done` as `volatile`, without any other changes to the code. We need to bear in mind that this is one of the few situations where access to shared mutable data does not have to be synchronised.

You may have read elsewhere that synchronisation is expensive in terms of performance and that it should be avoided whenever possible. Such advice is not only dangerous but also no longer valid. Although synchronisation was indeed rather slow in early JVM implementations, it is now much more efficient, especially in the vast majority of cases where there is no **contention**, i.e. only one thread is trying to acquire a lock.

4.2 Avoid unnecessary synchronisation

While avoiding synchronisation leads to race conditions, synchronising too much code may lead to deadlocks. An example is the **nested monitor lockout** situation which occurs when a thread T_1 blocks while holding the lock on some object obj, and the only way to unblock T_1 is for another thread T_2 to call some other method on obj. The two threads deadlock, because T_2 is waiting for T_1 to release the lock on obj, while T_1 is waiting for T_2 to execute the code that will unblock T_1. This may seem a rare and convoluted situation, but here is an innocently looking example adapted from Allen Holub (1998).

Programming Java threads in the real world.

```
import java.util.concurrent.BlockingQueue;

class DeadlockExample
{
    private BlockingQueue q = ... // initialisation

    // other fields and other methods that do not access q

    public synchronized void methodA(Object o)
    {
        // do some processing on the object
        q.put(o);
        // do something more
    }

    public synchronized void methodB()
    {
        Object o = q.take();
        // do something with the object
    }
}
```

Blocking queues are useful for *separate and independent* consumer and producer threads so that they can take and put elements into a shared queue in any scheduled order without having to worry about exceptions. However, the DeadlockExample class *centralises and serialises* access to a queue through a single object. This leads to deadlock, as the following scenario shows.

If thread T_1 executes methodB and q is empty, the thread will block, waiting on a notification that an item has been put into the queue. However, such an item can only be put by another thread T_2 calling methodA, but T_2 cannot obtain the lock on the DeadlockExample instance. The point is that when T_1 calls wait within take, it releases only the lock on q, not the lock on the DeadlockExample object (see *Unit 3*, Section 4). Both threads deadlock, each waiting for the other. Another deadlock scenario is for T_1 to call methodA on a full queue and then T_2 calls methodB.

If the two methods are synchronised because they access the shared queue, then we clearly have a case of excessive synchronisation because the synchronisation on q should be left to the BlockingQueue's methods. If the methods are synchronised for another reason, not shown in the code extract, then the code has to be changed, e.g. to provide another unsynchronised call to put, or to test whether the queue is empty before calling take, or to use a normal queue instead of a blocking one.

The general advice is that synchronised code should avoid calling methods outside its control, even if they are known not to block. Such calls may take a long time to execute, and since they are being executed while a lock is being held, no other thread can acquire the same lock. This leads to less potential concurrency and to a performance penalty. The ideal is therefore to obtain a lock, inspect the shared data, update it and release the lock, leaving any other operations outside the synchronised block of code.

4.3   Always call `wait` inside a loop

This advice basically states that a call to `wait` should always occur in the context

```
synchronized (obj)
{
  while (/*condition does not hold*/)
  {
    obj.wait();
  }
  // do something
}
```

or

```
// synchronized method signature
{
  // do something
  while (/*condition does not hold*/)
  {
    wait();
  }
  // do something
}
```

We have already come across this advice in *Unit 3*, Section 4, where we explained why `wait` has to be inside the loop.

SAQ 9

Why should the call to `wait` not be within a simple `if`?

ANSWER...

Typically, `o` is `this` (i.e. the current object) and we can, in such cases, just write `wait`.

When a thread *T* resumes execution after a call to `o.wait()`, this only means two things: *T* was notified by some other thread, and *T* has reacquired the lock on object `o`. In particular, resumption of execution does *not* mean that the condition has become true. For example, *T* might have been woken together with other threads by a `notifyAll`, and one of those threads may have acquired the lock on `o` first and invalidated the condition again.

The code for methods of the `BlockingQueue` interface in the discussion of Exercise 9 illustrates the reason given in the above answer. If the `take` method's first instruction were just an `if` statement

```
if (/*this queue is empty*/)
{
  wait();
}
```

the following scenario would be possible with an empty queue `q`.

1   Consumer thread C_1 gets the lock on `q`, calls `q.take()` and waits, releasing the lock.

2   Consumer thread C_2 does the same.

3   Producer thread P_1 gets the lock on q, calls q.put(o), which notifies the waiting threads C_1 and C_2, and then releases the lock.

4   C_1 becomes the running thread, reacquires the lock, resumes execution after the wait call, removes the element from the queue, notifies all waiting threads (but there are none), and releases the lock.

5   C_2 becomes the running thread, reacquires the lock, resumes execution after the wait call, and tries to remove an element from an empty queue, which leads to an error.

If we had used the while loop instead, C_2 would have had to recheck the condition in step 5, and wait again for the queue to become non-empty.

4.4 Do not depend on the thread scheduler

This advice should not come as a surprise after Subsection 2.4. Correct and portable programs should depend on the absence of race conditions and on proper communication of values among threads, not on tweaking thread priorities and calling yield to force a particular execution order, nor on assuming that threads are always pre-empted.

If you find yourself tempted to give higher priority to some threads in order to increase the responsiveness of the system, keep in mind that the best way to achieve a responsive application is to have only a few runnable threads at any time. This can be achieved mainly by the way you allocate threads to the tasks your application has to perform. In cases where many threads are unavoidable, the way to keep the number of runnable ones low is to have each one do as little as necessary and then wait on some condition or sleep for some time. This also avoids starvation of other threads in the case where the underlying threading model is cooperative.

However, Bloch mentions one situation where using yield can be useful, namely during testing in order to artificially increase the concurrency of the application and hence test it under heavier contention rates.

4.5 Document thread safety

The previous points of advice help to make a class **thread-safe**. A class is considered thread-safe if its instances behave under concurrent method calls as if they were called sequentially. In other words, it is not possible for a multithreaded application to observe an instance of that class in an incoherent state, i.e. a state that could not be observed by a single-threaded application. **Thread safety** is an important property in guaranteeing expected behaviour, but it is not always desirable or possible to make a class completely thread-safe.

A situation where it is not desirable to have a thread-safe class is when instances of that class are likely to be accessed hundreds or thousands of times within a single-threaded application (or by a single thread within a multithreaded application). An example is a class that implements a commonly used data structure: typically, there will be many accesses to add, remove or retrieve data elements. Imposing thread safety in such a case means that each access is synchronised. Although synchronisation under no contention is efficient, it does have some overhead, and over many accesses a performance penalty may be noticed. It is therefore preferable to provide two versions of such classes, one that is thread-safe and one that is not, for use by single threads. The thread-safe class may wrap or subclass the other one. The Java Collections Framework has taken the wrapping approach for some of the collection data structures, as we have seen in Subsection 3.2.

A situation where it is impossible to make the class thread-safe is when a thread is allowed to inspect an instance while other threads modify it. Again, a good example stems from the Collections Framework: one thread may iterate over the collection while another modifies it. To ensure correct behaviour, the iterating code should be synchronised on the collection, as we have seen in Subsection 3.2.

As the last example shows, sometimes the correct behaviour cannot be guaranteed solely by **internal synchronisation**, i.e. synchronisation performed by the class's methods; it also requires **external synchronisation**, i.e. synchronisation performed by the method callers.

The previous discussion shows that thread safety is not an 'all or nothing' property: some classes that are not thread-safe can still be used in multithreaded settings with some adaptations. It is therefore paramount that developers document the level of thread safety supported by the classes they implement. This will tell clients if they can use the class in a multithreaded setting or not, and if they can, whether external synchronisation is needed. You must also be aware that the `synchronized` modifier is considered in Java to be an implementation detail; as such, it does not show up in the documentation generated by Javadoc. This reinforces the need for properly documenting the thread safety of each class.

Bloch identified the following levels of thread safety a class can support.

Immutable classes

Immutable classes have instances that remain constant to client threads. Therefore, no external synchronisation is needed. An example of an immutable class is `java.lang.String`: there is no method to change an already existing string.

Thread-safe classes

Thread-safe classes have mutable instances, but internal synchronisation performed by the class's methods imposes sequential access to the data. Many of the classes given as examples in this course are thread-safe because all their data access methods are synchronised.

Conditionally thread-safe classes

Conditionally thread-safe classes require a sequence of accesses to be invoked without interference. Hence the client has to put such a sequence of calls within a synchronised block of code. The documentation should indicate which calls need to be externally synchronised. An example of a conditionally thread-safe class is `Vector`: accesses to a vector are synchronised, but to iterate safely over a vector, it has to be locked – the Java 1.5 API documentation said:

See the Javadoc for details of the API for the `Vector` class.

Capitalisation, spelling and italics as in the original.

> The Iterators returned by `Vector`'s `iterator` and `listIterator` methods are *fail-fast*: if the Vector is structurally modified at any time after the Iterator is created, in any way except through the Iterator's own `remove` or `add` methods, the Iterator will throw a `ConcurrentModificationException`. [...] Note that the fail-fast behavior of an iterator cannot be guaranteed as it is, generally speaking, impossible to make any hard guarantees in the presence of unsynchronized concurrent modification. Fail-fast iterators throw `ConcurrentModificationException` on a best-effort basis. Therefore, it would be wrong to write a program that depended on this exception for its correctness: *the fail-fast behavior of iterators should be used only to detect bugs.*

Iterating over a vector therefore requires external synchronisation in order to avoid any exceptions, as we have seen in Subsection 3.2:

```
synchronized (v)
{
  for (Iterator i = v.iterator(); i.hasNext(); )
  {
  // do something on i.next()
  }
}
```

The Java documentation quoted above might give the impression that it's only the use of iterators that may lead to problems. However, other ways of accessing the collection must also be externally synchronised, including seemingly innocuous expressions such as $v.get(v.size() - 1)$. Without synchronising on v, the following might happen:

1   thread T_1 computes the size of the vector v;

2   T_1 is pre-empted by another thread that removes an element of the vector;

3   T_1 regains CPU control and tries to access the last element of the vector, thereby throwing an `ArrayIndexOutOfBoundsException`.

The general rule is simple: if two consecutive synchronised method calls (like `hasNext` and `next`, or `size` and `get`) might have unexpected results if a concurrent modification occurs between the two calls, then the class is not thread-safe, only conditionally so.

Thread-compatible classes

Thread-compatible classes do not use internal synchronisation and hence require external synchronisation for most method calls or sequences of method calls. An example of a thread-compatible class is `ArrayList`, a kind of unsynchronised version of `Vector` – the Java 1.5 documentation said:

See the Javadoc for details of the API for the `ArrayList` class.

> **Note that this implementation is not synchronized**. If multiple threads access an `ArrayList` instance concurrently, and at least one of the threads modifies the list structurally, it *must* be synchronized externally. (A structural modification is any operation that adds or deletes one or more elements, or explicitly resizes the backing array; merely setting the value of an element is not a structural modification.)

Bold, italics and spelling as in the original.

`ArrayList` objects should therefore be mostly used in single-threaded applications. However, if concurrent access is needed, there are several options to achieve it. If there are not many accesses in the application code, and only a few of the class methods are used, it might be easiest to synchronise each access:

```
synchronize (anArrayList)
{
  // some method call on anArrayList
}
```

If, however, most of the class methods are called, it might be easier to access the `ArrayList` object via synchronised methods of another object. This is similar to a `DeadlockExample` object encapsulating a `BlockingQueue` object. The difference is that `ArrayList` methods are neither synchronised nor block, and therefore encapsulating an array list within another object is not unnecessary synchronisation and it will not lead to deadlock.

SAQ 10

What is the simplest way of accessing 'the `ArrayList` object via synchronised methods', as suggested above?

ANSWER..

The simplest way is to wrap it using `Collections.synchronizedList` (Subsection 3.2).

Activity 4.5

Thread-hostile example.

Thread-hostile classes

Thread-hostile classes are not safe to use within multithreaded applications, even if externally synchronising each method call. A common reason is that thread-hostile classes change static data: even if synchronising all instance methods, different threads holding locks on different instances can change the static data concurrently. The solution is to have synchronised static methods, as you can see in the activity.

For most of the cases, the name of the thread-safety level is enough for developers to know whether external synchronisation is needed or not, but conditionally thread-safe (and possibly thread-compatible) classes have to document exactly in which cases external synchronisation is needed. The best way is to provide concrete examples on how to call the relevant methods, as we have done above.

SAQ 11

What are the thread-safety levels of `LinkedList` and `CopyOnWriteArrayList` mentioned in Subsection 3.2?

ANSWER..

`LinkedList` is thread-compatible, like `ArrayList`, while `CopyOnWriteArrayList` is conditionally thread-safe. The latter is not thread-safe because different threads may see the data structure in different states due to the weakly consistent iterators.

A final word of warning on thread safety: although Bloch was a Distinguished Engineer at Sun Microsystems, his thread-safety levels were not adopted in the Javadoc API documentation. Instead, more informal terms like 'synchronised class' or 'unsynchronised version' are used, as we have done in Subsection 3.2 before we had the more rigorous terminology available. Moreover, 'thread-safe' is often used in the API documentation in a general sense that includes other thread-safety levels.

4.6 Summary of advice on code writing

This section has presented advice to avoid some common problems when developing concurrent programs. The main points to keep in mind are the following.

► The main advice is to synchronise all code that accesses shared mutable data, because synchronisation imposes the mutual exclusion and memory barriers that are necessary for the memory model to guarantee the correct execution of the code. In some exceptional cases, where mutual exclusion is guaranteed and only the memory barriers have to be added, it's possible to just use volatile variables.

► However, synchronising too much code may lead to deadlock. One such situation is the nested monitor lockout. In general, the best approach is for synchronised code to do as little as possible, namely to just read or update the shared data. Any further activity, especially if it is time consuming or depends on calling methods that may block, should be done while not holding a lock.

▶ Incorrect behaviour may also occur if the precondition for executing some synchronised code is not retested after a waiting thread resumes execution. To avoid such problems, the `wait` call should be inside a loop that exits only when the precondition is true.

▶ The execution of programs should not depend on the underlying threading model. Threads should do only the strictly necessary and then sleep or wait for some condition. This reduces the number of runnable threads at any point in time, making the program more responsive and reducing the possibility of starvation in cooperative multitasking.

▶ A class is considered thread-safe if it behaves correctly under multiple concurrent accesses. There are various levels of thread safety: immutable, thread-safe, conditionally thread-safe, thread-compatible and thread-hostile. Conditionally thread-safe and thread-compatible classes require all method calls or some sequences of calls to be externally synchronised. The thread-safety level of a class should be explicitly documented so that developers know whether the class can be used in concurrent applications, and, if so, whether external synchronisation is needed and in which cases.

5 Summary

In this unit we have taken a closer look at Java's support for concurrency and at subtle issues that arise in concurrent programs.

We started with a brief description of the JVM. A virtual machine is an abstract computational device that allows code generated for such a machine to be run on every platform for which a corresponding interpreter exists. This makes programs more portable, but their execution is slower than if compiled directly to machine code. However, virtual machines are not a panacea for portability because programs may still depend on the target platform's resources (e.g. memory and display capacities). This explains why there are various JVM specifications for the different Java editions. We have seen that the JVM includes a class loader, a bytecode verifier and a garbage collector, that some memory areas are local to each thread, and that implementations may incorporate optimisation techniques, like JIT compilation, to speed up execution.

Java was the first mainstream language to incorporate cross-platform memory and threading models into the language specification. The aim of such models is to ensure that a concurrent program can exhibit the same behaviour on different platforms. However, if Java threads are mapped to native OS threads, the program's behaviour will depend on the underlying scheduling and prioritisation policies. We have also seen that mutual exclusion may solve some subtle problems like code reordering, but that this is not in itself enough to ensure correctness of concurrent programs. Additionally, memory barriers are necessary to ensure consistent shared data. Memory barriers are enforced by the `synchronized` and `volatile` constructs.

Unfortunately, Java's built-in concurrency support is rather low-level and has its limitations, including only a single implicit condition variable per lock and no possibility of retracting lock acquisition attempts. Java 1.5 introduced a concurrency utilities library that provides, among other things, collection classes that perform better under concurrency but enforce less strict consistency requirements and configurable task-execution services, based on thread pools. All this allows developers to use efficient code developed by concurrency experts, instead of spending time reinventing the wheel.

Using library classes requires us to know exactly which of the various levels of thread safety they support. In practical terms, we need to know whether certain calls or sequences of calls have to be externally synchronised. Likewise, we need to document the thread-safety level of the classes we develop, and make sure we avoid some common pitfalls of multithreaded programming.

LEARNING OUTCOMES

When you have completed your study of this unit you should be able to do the following:

▶ explain what a virtual machine is and state its advantages and disadvantages;

▶ explain what the Java Virtual Machine does;

▶ explain the threats to portability of Java programs;

▶ explain the difference between mutual exclusion and memory barrier, the problems which each technique addresses and how the two techniques are built into Java;

▶ explain some of the limitations of Java's built-in concurrency mechanisms and how the new concurrency utilities address them;

▶ write simple programs using some of the concurrency utilities introduced in Java 1.5: concurrent collections, atomic variables, locks and associated conditions, semaphores, and thread pools;

▶ discuss the impact on performance and correctness of various solutions to a given concurrency problem;

▶ explain the various levels of thread safety, and, given the code of a class, recognise which level it supports;

▶ write thread-safe, portable Java programs, following the advice given throughout the unit, and, conversely, recognise potential concurrency and portability problems in given code fragments.

Glossary

bytecode   The 'machine code' of the Java Virtual Machine, i.e. the result of compiling a Java program.

bytecode verifier   The part of the Java Virtual Machine that checks whether the bytecode about to be executed has not been tampered with.

class loader   A part of the Java Virtual Machine that loads classes at runtime into the Java Virtual Machine's memory. Java developers can implement their own specialised class loaders.

conditionally thread-safe class   A class that requires some external synchronisation to achieve thread safety. For example, individual accesses may not need external synchronisation, but a sequence of them might.

contention   A situation in which multiple threads are attempting to obtain the same resource.

countdown latch   A flexible thread-coordination mechanism that makes one group of threads wait for each of N other threads to reach a certain point in their execution, with N being the initial value of the latch's counter.

divide-and-conquer strategy   A problem-solving strategy that breaks down a problem into subproblems of the same or similar type, continuing the process until the obtained subproblems are simple enough to be solved directly.

external synchronisation   Synchronisation done by the callers of methods.

factory method   A method that creates objects. Typically, a factory method is a static method that hides the concrete class of the returned object: the client knows only which interface the object implements.

fail-fast operation   An operation that fails as soon as it detects some violation to consistency invariants. For example, iterators over pre-Java 1.5 collections throw an exception as soon as they detect that another thread is modifying the collection.

garbage collection   A runtime technique to free the memory occupied by objects that are no longer used. The Java Virtual Machine specification does not impose any specific garbage collection algorithm.

green thread   A thread that is not visible to the operating system and has to be created, scheduled and terminated by the Java Virtual Machine.

immutable class   A thread-safe class whose instances never change once they have been created.

internal synchronisation   Synchronisation done by the methods themselves.

interpreter   A program that executes another program.

Java Virtual Machine (JVM)   A virtual machine defined mainly with the execution of Java programs in mind. The Java Virtual Machine is a specification, and there are many implementations of it, optimised for different platforms or Java editions.

just-in-time (JIT) compilation   A technique to compile a sequence of virtual machine instructions into machine code as the sequence is being executed.

master–slave model A model of communication in which one device or process (the master) has unidirectional control over other devices or processes (the slaves). For example, in a client–server system, the client is the master and the server is the slave.

memory barrier A special instruction to make local and shared memories consistent with each other.

memory model A specification of how and when updates to shared data have to be propagated across different memories and processes.

native thread A thread visible to the operating system and scheduled by it.

nested monitor lockout A situation in which a thread T blocks or waits while holding a lock on the monitor that would enable other threads to make T progress. Thread T has therefore locked itself inside the monitor, keeping the 'key', i.e. the monitor's lock.

priority queue A queue that orders elements according to their associated priority so that the next element to be removed from the queue has the highest priority.

scalability under contention The ability of an algorithm to maintain a high throughput under contention, i.e. to keep a high ratio of number of threads per time unit that access the same resource.

thread pool A set of threads, each one taking a task from a common queue, executing it and then fetching the next task. The main aim of the pool is to reuse threads for multiple tasks, in order to optimise the memory usage and the performance of the application.

thread safety The property of a class behaving under concurrent access in the same way as under sequential execution. There are various levels of thread safety, depending on how much external synchronisation is necessary to achieve it.

thread-compatible class A class that provides no internal synchronisation. As such, access to it requires external synchronisation within a concurrent application.

thread-hostile class A class that is not safe to use in concurrent programs. No amount of external synchronisation will make instances of such classes behave as if they were accessed sequentially.

thread-safe class A class that has mutable instances and where the effect of any concurrent access to an instance could also be obtained by some sequential execution. Thread-safe classes do not require any external synchronisation.

virtual machine (VM) An abstract computing device implemented in software. A virtual machine defines a certain set of instructions and how code and data are organised in the machine's memory.

volatile variable A variable declared with the `volatile` modifier. For practical purposes it is as if such variables are always accessed directly in shared memory. Moreover, an access to a volatile variable creates a memory barrier.

weakly consistent operation An operation that does not guarantee consistency invariants and as such does not fail under concurrent accesses. The iterators returned by the concurrency classes introduced in Java 1.5 are weakly consistent and never throw a exception due to concurrent modification.

wrapper method   A method that adds new functionality or properties to existing objects. The `Collections` class provides static wrapper methods to turn thread-compatible collections into conditionally thread-safe ones.

References

Bloch, J. (2001) *Effective Java*, Addison-Wesley.

Holub, A. (1998) *Programming Java threads in the real world, Part 2* [online], http://www.javaworld.com/javaworld/jw-10-1998/jw-10-toolbox.html?page=1 (Accessed 19 September 2007).

Lea, D. (1999) *Concurrent Programming in Java: Design Principles and Patterns* (2nd edn), Addison-Wesley.

Manson, J. and Goetz, B. (2004) *JSR 133 (Java Memory Model) FAQ* [online], http://www.cs.umd.edu/~pugh/java/memoryModel/jsr-133-faq.html (Accessed 5 September 2007).

McConnell, S. (2004) *Code Complete* (2nd edn), Microsoft Press.

Montfort, N. (2005) *Twisty Little Passages*, MIT Press.

Index

A

activation frame 10

B

bytecode 7
    verifier 10

C

cache flush 19

cache invalidation 19

class
    `ArrayList` 28–30, 49–50
    `CopyOnWriteArrayList` 29, 50
    `CountDownLatch` 38–39
    `LinkedList` 28, 50
    `ReentrantLock` 34–37
    `Semaphore` 37–38
    `ThreadPoolExecutor` 41–42

class file format 9–10

class loader 10

code reordering 13

condition variable 25

conditionally thread-safe class 48

contention 33, 36, 44, 47

cooperative multitasking 51

countdown latch 38–39

D

divide-and-conquer strategy 40

E

example
    `CarPark` 38
    `Counter` 32
    `DeadlockExample` 45
    `MyThread` 18, 44
    `Reordering` 14, 16
    `VolatileExample` 20

exception
    `ArrayIndexOutOfBoundsException` 49
    `ConcurrentModificationException` 29, 48
    `IllegalMonitorStateException` 37
    `IndexOutOfBoundsException` 27
    `NoSuchElementException` 29
    `RejectedExecutionException` 41

F

factory method 41

fail-fast iterator 29, 48

G

garbage collection 11

H

heap 10

hot spot 11

I

immutable class 48

interface
    `BlockingQueue` 30–31, 36, 45–46, 49
    `Collection` 26
    `Condition` 33, 35–37
    `ExecutorService` 41–42
    `List` 26
    `Lock` 33–37
    `Queue` 30

interpreter 6

J

Java Collections Framework 26

Java Community Process 25

Java Enterprise Edition 12

Java Micro Edition 12

Java Platform 12

Java Specification Request 25

Java Standard Edition 12

Java Virtual Machine (JVM) 7

just-in-time (JIT) compilation 9

L

latch 38

M

master–slave model 40

memory
    area 10
    barrier 19
    model 19

method area 10

mutual exclusion 16, 52

N
native thread 52

nested monitor lockout 45, 50

P
priority
    boosting 23
    queue 30

producer–consumer 31

program counter 10

S
scalability under contention 33

semaphore 37

synchronisation
    internal 48
    external 48

T
test-and-set operation 31

thread
    green 22
    native 22
    pool 40
    priority 25, 47
    safety 5, 43

threading model 51

thread-compatible class 49

thread-hostile class 50

thread-safe class 47–48

thread-safety level 51

V
virtual machine (VM) 6

volatile variable 17, 19

W
weakly consistent iterator 29

wrapper method 29, 56